DoubleVision

Katalog unterstützt von
Catalogue funded by

**The Henry Moore
Foundation**

DoubleVision

The British Council

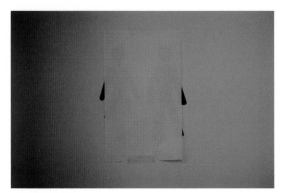

Richard Wentworth, BERLIN – 117 LANDMARKS / MARKSTEINE

Das Berliner Künstlerprogramm des Deutschen Akademischen Austauschdienstes kann in diesem Jahr auf eine 35jährige Tätigkeit zurückblicken, in der Musiker, Literaten, Film-Autoren und Bildende Künstler in Berlin zu Gast waren. Dieses bietet Anlass, auf einige ausgewählte Aspekte der zurückliegenden Ereignisse genauer zu schauen, um festzustellen, dass in der Tat Geschichte geschrieben wurde. So verhält es sich, wenn man auf die letzten Jahre zurückblickt, die ganz wesentlich von der Anwesenheit britischer Künstler in Berlin geprägt waren. Alle waren da, so könnte man es zusammenfassen, und sie waren gekommen, als die ganz große Aufmerksamkeit eben noch schlummerte. Das ist schon eine kleine Sensation, wenn man sich die Gästeliste vergegenwärtigt, aus der Andrea Schlieker die Ausstellung DOUBLE VISION für die Galerie für Zeitgenössische Kunst Leipzig konzipiert hat.

Der Focus auf diesen Austausch zwischen Großbritannien und Berlin macht deutlich, wie sehr das Prinzip Austausch, verbunden mit der Bereitschaft, sich auf eine fremde Umgebung und deren Erkundung einzulassen, sowohl künstlerisches wie auch gesellschaftliches Potential enthält, kulturelle und politische Dialoge zu prägen. DOUBLE VISION ist ein Beispiel dafür. Der Aufenthalt von Rachel Whiteread in Berlin gab den Anlass, sich intensiv mit dem Thema Holocaust auseinanderzusetzen, eine Grundlage für ihr in Wien realisiertes Denkmal für den Judenplatz. Aber auch in anderen, weniger spektakulären Werken tritt das Moment eines fremden, neuen Blicks vor Augen. Hier liegt eine Bedeutungsebene des Ausstellungstitels DOUBLE VISION, der den Dialog zum Prinzip erhebt.

Wie das DAAD-Programm selbst, so ist auch die Ausstellung Resultat einer Kooperation, obwohl in diesem Fall von drei Institutionen: dem DAAD, dem British Council und der Galerie für Zeitgenössische Kunst in Leipzig. Alle drei Institutionen waren am Entstehungsprozess der Ausstellung beteiligt. Wir möchten zunächst den Künstlern danken, ohne deren Vision eine doppelte erst gar nicht möglich gewesen wäre. Wir danken Andrea Schlieker für das außergewöhnliche Engagement, das nicht zuletzt die Fortsetzung ihrer siebenjährigen Jurytätigkeit für das Berliner Künstlerprogramm mit anderen Mitteln spiegelt. Unser Dank gilt ebenso der Henry Moore Foundation für die Bereitstellung von Mitteln für diesen Katalog.

Wir freuen uns, dass der ursprüngliche Dialog, der mit Gastaufenthalten in Berlin und später Hannover und München einmal seinen Anfang nahm, mit dieser Ausstellung so erweitert werden kann, dass eine weitere bedeutende deutsche Stadt in den Radius gegenseitiger Erkundung und Erfahrung aufgenommen wird.

Ulrich Podewils, DAAD, Berlin
Andrea Rose, British Council, London
Barbara Steiner, Galerie für Zeitgenössische Kunst, Leipzig

Andrea Schlieker

Parallele Begegnungen an verschiedenen Orten*

* Der Titel dieses Aufsatzes ist einer Arbeit von Stephen Willats entlehnt, die er in der GAK in Bremen 1998 zeigte.

Seit Ende der achtziger Jahre steht die junge britische Kunstszene im Brennpunkt des Interesses und findet internationale Anerkennung. Weltweit gefeiert, erfindet sie sich selbst ständig neu und zeigt dabei keinerlei Anzeichen, ihren Schwung zu verlieren. Kein anderes Land erfreut sich auf dem internationalen Parkett der zeitgenössischen Ausstellungspraxis seit über einem Jahrzehnt derart anhaltender Aufmerksamkeit. Davon zeugte im Lauf der neunziger Jahre eine fortgesetzte Reihe von Ausstellungen wie etwa WITH ATTITUDE (Brüssel, 1992), BRILLIANT! (Minneapolis, 1995), MINKY MANKY (London, 1995), LIFE/LIVE (Paris und Lissabon, 1995), FULL HOUSE (Wolfsburg, 1996), PICTURA BRITANNICA (Sydney, 1997) oder SENSATION (London, Berlin und New York, 1997-2000), um nur einige zu nennen.

Künstler betrachten nationale Ausstellungen allerdings oft mit Argwohn, meiden sie sogar, weil sie ihre Arbeiten lieber im größeren internationalen Kontext sehen. In den letzten Jahren haben sich britische Künstler immer öfter geweigert, unter dem groß vermarkteten Etikett YBA ('young British artists') auszustellen, weil sie das Gefühl hatten, durch diesen eng gefassten Begriff könnte ihr Werk in einen glatten Slogan verflacht

und in einer hochgejubelten „Sensations"-Verpackung leicht konsumierbar gemacht werden, die über ihre komplexen und vielschichtigen Identitäten, Geschichten und Ziele hinwegtäuscht.

DOUBLE VISION geht über die wohlbekannte YBA-Formel hinaus: Die fünfzehn hier gezeigten Künstlerinnen und Künstler präsentieren ein breiteres, generationsübergreifendes Spektrum der britischen Kunstlandschaft. Eins ist ihnen jedoch gemeinsam: Alle haben in Deutschland gelebt und gearbeitet, größtenteils in Berlin, als Gäste des angesehenen DAAD-Künstlerprogramms. Ihr Aufenthalt – ob nun für ein paar Monate oder ein ganzes Jahr – führte immer zu einem fruchtbaren Dialog zwischen den Künstlern und der Stadt ihrer Wahl, setzte dabei frische Energien und Inspirationen frei und bot ihnen einen neuen, unschätzbaren „doppelten" Blick, der oft unauslöschliche Spuren in ihrem Werk hinterließ.

Großbritannien war immer geprägt von seiner sorgfältig gepflegten Inselhaltung. Aus historischen wie geographischen Gründen darauf bedacht, die Trennung vom „Kontinent" aufrecht zu erhalten, hat sich das Land damit begnügt, auf ewig in einer „splendid isolation" zu verharren und diesen Eindruck auch nach außen zu ver-

mitteln (noch immer nennen die Briten den Rest von Europa distanziert den „Kontinent"). Erst in den letzten fünfzehn Jahren etwa lässt sich eine allmähliche Öffnung feststellen und wird ein immer noch zögerliches Gefühl der Identifizierung mit den europäischen Nachbarn spürbar. Aus diesem Klima kultureller Selbstbeobachtung heraus bot das DAAD-Künstlerprogramm eine wichtige Brücke, über die britische Künstler – oft zum ersten Mal im Leben – in ein anderes Land kamen, um hier zu leben und zu arbeiten und in eine fremde Kultur, Sprache und Politik einzutauchen. Für viele war es eine Offenbarung, die ihnen nicht nur andere Lebensstile eröffnete, sondern auch den kritischen, objektivierenden Abstand von ihrem akzeptierten Gefühl nationaler Identität vermittelte. Der Zeitraum, in dem sie in Deutschland lebten und arbeiteten, wurde für sie zu einer wichtigen Markierung in ihrer Laufbahn, manchmal sogar zu einem Wendepunkt. Nationale Stereotypen lösen sich in einen anderen Kontext auf, die chauvinistische Nabelschau weicht einer breiteren Perspektive.

DOUBLE VISION, eine Ausstellung, die Malerei, Skulptur, Photographie und Installation sowie Sound-, Film- und Videoarbeiten umfasst, zeigt die Werke von einigen der seit langem maßgeblichen Vertreter der zeitgenössischen britischen Kunstszene. Die Auswahl von fünfzehn (aus über vierzig) britischen Künstlerinnen und Künstlern, die seit Mitte der sechziger Jahre in den Genuss des Künstlerprogramms gekommen sind, bietet mit dem breiten Spektrum von Generationen, Bekanntheitsgrad und verwendeten Medien gleichzeitig einen repräsentativen Querschnitt durch die aktuelle britische Kunstgeschichte.

Obgleich einige der ausgestellten Werke sich ganz direkt auf die während des Auslandaufenthalts gemachten Erfahrungen beziehen, schien es zu restriktiv und pedantisch, dies zum entscheidenden Kriterium für die Auswahl zu erheben – zumal eine Reihe von diesen schon mehrfach ausgestellt waren. Es war stattdessen wichtiger, mit ganz neuen oder kürzlich entstandenen Werken das aktuelle Schaffen zu repräsentieren.

Die Vielfalt der künstlerischen Positionen sowie ihre gemeinsame Verwurzelung im DAAD-Stipendienprogramm versagt sich einer streng thematisch ausgerichteten Ausstellung, doch lassen sich in der Freiheit einer nicht chronologischen Lesart eine Reihe von verbindenden Motiven finden, die die verschiedenen Exponate

GOOD ENVIRONMENT FOR
MONOCHROME COLOURED PAINTINGS,
daadgalerie 1994

durchziehen und an Stelle einer einzigen geradlinigen Argumentation ein Netzwerk aus Querverweisen und Gegenüberstellungen bilden.

Damien Hirst, zweifellos der bekannteste unter den Künstlern des so genannten „Brit-Pack", wird mit seinen extravaganten, theatralischen Aktionen identifiziert, bei denen er ganze Kühe und Schweine in Scheiben schneidet, um sie dann in Formaldehydlösung zu konservieren. Hirst war derjenige, der 1988 mit seiner mittlerweile legendären Ausstellung FREEZE das Phänomen YBA ins Leben rief. Mit genialer kuratorischer Finesse und großem Gespür für die Kunst, sich in Szene zu setzen, bot Hirst die Plattform, von der aus seine Künstlerkollegen ihre internationale Karriere starteten und Hirst (der zu dem Zeitpunkt einige ziemlich bescheidene farbige, konstruktivistische Kästen zeigte) ironischerweise hinter sich ließen.

Erst 1990, nach seiner spektakulären Präsentation von A THOUSAND YEARS (seiner ersten, ziemlich opernhaften Reflexion über den ewigen Kreislauf von Geburt und Tod, dargestellt am Beispiel von Fliegen, die sich in einem Kuhschädel vermehren und schließlich von einem

„insectocutor", einer Art Fliegentötungsmaschine, vernichtet werden) verschob sich das Zentrum des Interesses wieder. Seitdem hat Hirst sein Talent, für Überraschungen zu sorgen, immer wieder unter Beweis gestellt. Er hat sich in die Bereiche Film, Design und Werbung vorgewagt, dabei jedoch immer standhaft an seiner zentralen Position festgehalten. Trotz der Kaleidoskopartigkeit seiner Arbeiten sind sich bestimmte formale Elemente innerhalb der Parameter ständig wechselnder Variationen immer gleich geblieben, wie etwa seine „spot paintings" und seine Vitrinen, von denen in DOUBLE VISION jeweils Beispiele zu sehen sind. Ganz gleich, ob er tote Kühe oder lebende exotische Schmetterlinge verwendet, immer gelingt es Hirst, seinem unorthodoxen, organischen Material sowohl Instinktives und Aggressives wie Romantisches und Lyrisches zu entlocken. Ihm geht es um die beharrliche und immer wieder überraschende Erforschung seiner Lieblingsthemen Liebe und Tod.

Der Aufenthalt in Berlin 1994 kam zu einem entscheidenden Zeitpunkt in Hirsts Laufbahn und festigte seinen internationalen Ruf. „Ich liebe Berlin, und Berlin liebt mich" (der Beuyssche Titel in leicht abgewandelter Form) wäre die griffige Formel für seine dort verbrachte

NAJA NAJA KAOUTHIA, 2000
household gloss on canvas,
246 x 251.5 cm
Courtesy of Science ltd.

11 YIKES, 1997, glass, MDF and
drug packaging, 38 x 76 cm,
Courtesy Jay Jopling

12/13 STRIPTEASER, 1996
glass/steel wall cabinet
six parts filled with skeletons and
surgical instruments
195.2 x 420 x 48 cm
Collection of the artist

Zeit, die in der dramatischen Rauminstallation eines Schmetterlings-Korridors in der daadgalerie ihren Höhepunkt fand.

In DOUBLE VISION ist Hirsts kontinuierliche Beschäftigung mit Vergänglichkeit und der *condition humaine* in der Gestalt eines großen Wandschranks aus Glas und Stahl verkörpert: STRIPTEASER (1996), enthält zwei menschliche Skelette (aus Kunststoff) und ein Sortiment an chirurgischen Instrumenten. In WHEN LOGICS DIE, einer ziemlich grausigen, drastischen Anspielung auf Selbstmord, verwendete Hirst 1991 erstmals chirurgische Instrumente. Die Skelette, vermutlich ein männliches und ein weibliches, die jeweils isoliert voneinander in ihren gläsernen Särgen hängen und im Tod mit zwei Doppelvitrinen voller moderner medizinischer Utensilien verbunden sind (ähnlich den Grabgaben bei antiken Begräbnisriten), kommentieren auf sachlich-nüchterne und doch melancholische Weise die Themen Flüchtigkeit und Vergänglichkeit.

Regalsysteme mit säuberlich zur Schau gestellten Gegenständen – ob schön (Fische, Gläser, Muscheln) oder abstoßend (Zigarettenkippen, tierische Organe) – finden sich in Hirsts Werk häufig und verraten (ähnlich

wie bei seinen Altersgenossen Douglas Gordon und Simon Patterson) seine Faszination für Taxonomien und Klassifizierungssysteme. Wie seine klaustrophobischen Glas-und-Stahl-Kästen fungieren auch diese Wandbehälter als modernes *memento mori* und erinnern uns an die Vergänglichkeit des Lebens und unsere matten Versuche, es zu verkürzen oder zu verlängern.

Dualismen wie Leben und Tod, Gut und Böse, Liebe und Hass liegen auch vielen Arbeiten von **Douglas Gordon** zugrunde. Für die Skulpturen-Projekte 1997 in Münster zum Beispiel stellte der Künstler zwei bekannte Kinogeschichten in einer dunklen, feuchten Fußgängerunterführung einander gegenüber – DAS LIED DER BERNADETTE und DER EXORZIST. Indem er beide Filme gleichzeitig von beiden Seiten auf eine einzige Leinwand projizierte, verschmolz er im übertragenen wie im wortwörtlichen Sinn Himmel und Hölle miteinander.

Gordon ist in Leipzig kein Unbekannter. Er hat sein filmisches Werk hier bereits zweimal gezeigt: Man erinnere sich an 1995, als sein mittlerweile legendärer Film 24 HOUR PSYCHO in der riesigen Halle des Leipziger Hauptbahnhofs vorgeführt wurde. Mit dieser verlang-

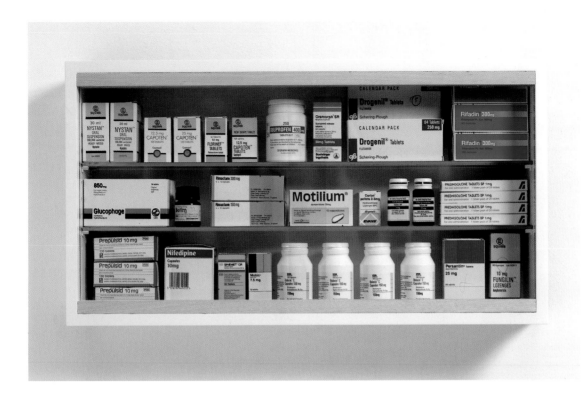

samten, ohne Ton gespielten Fassung von Hitchcocks Klassiker begann seine internationale Laufbahn.

Durch die Manipulation von gefundenem Filmmaterial (darunter medizinisches Archivmaterial oder ausgemusterte Teile von beliebten Fernsehserien) legt Gordon unerwartete Bedeutungsschichten frei. Unverhoffte psychologische Nuancen, erotische Zweideutigkeiten oder moralische Zwangslagen entfalten sich aus verlangsamt und tonlos abgespielten, appropriierten Filmfragmenten.

Die Betonung persönlicher oder kollektiver Erinnerung stellt einen weiteren wichtigen Aspekt in Gordons Werk dar. Er erforscht ihn nicht nur in seinen Film- und Videoarbeiten, sondern auch in seinen zahlreichen Text- und Aktionsarbeiten. Mit LIST OF NAMES (1990 begonnen), einer epischen, ständig anwachsenden Wandzeichnung, auf der die Namen sämtlicher Menschen aufgelistet sind, denen begegnet zu sein Gordon sich erinnert, fixiert er flüchtige Erinnerung durch Text. Andere Arbeiten wie SOMETHING BETWEEN MY MOUTH AND YOUR EAR (1994) und WORDS AND PICTURES (1996, anlässlich von MOVING IMAGES 1999 in Leipzig gezeigt), erreichten dies durch die Verwendung von Sound (Musik) bzw. Bild (Film).

Wie seine Altersgenossen Damien Hirst und Mat Collishaw stellt Gordon (simulierte) Gewalt und Erotik bei einigen Werken in den Vordergrund, setzt sich mit ihnen allerdings vielleicht etwas spielerischer, ironischer oder „psychologisierender" auseinander (vgl. DIVIDED SELF, 1996). In seinem Soundwerk WHAT YOU WANT ME TO SAY (1998) kann man den Künstler über ein Dutzend willkürlich im Raum aufgestellte Lautsprecher „I love you" murmeln hören. Der psychologisch aufschlussreiche Titel untergräbt sofort den Glauben an die Botschaft und sabotiert jeden Eindruck von Glaubwürdigkeit. Und doch scheint es unmöglich, der hypnotisierenden Verlockung des wiederholten Bekenntnisses nicht zu erliegen. Dieses ironische Spiel mit unserer Sehnsucht, zu lieben und geliebt zu werden (sogar jenseits aller Vernunft und bis hin zur Selbsttäuschung) erhält ihre typisch scharfe, beißende Form auch in Damien Hirsts I'LL LOVE YOU FOREVER (1994): eine Stahlvitrine mit Vorhängeschloss, darin eine Gasmaske und medizinische Abfälle in aufgereihten, grellbunten Eimern mit der großformatigen Aufschrift „Gefahr".

Den Begriff „Innenräume/Intérieurs" und deren Bedeutung und Definition untersuchen auf ganz unter-

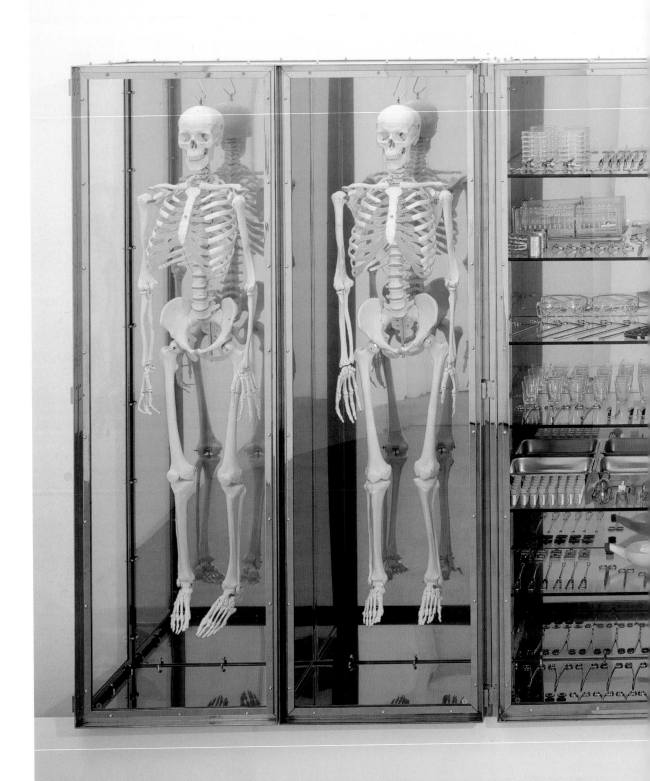

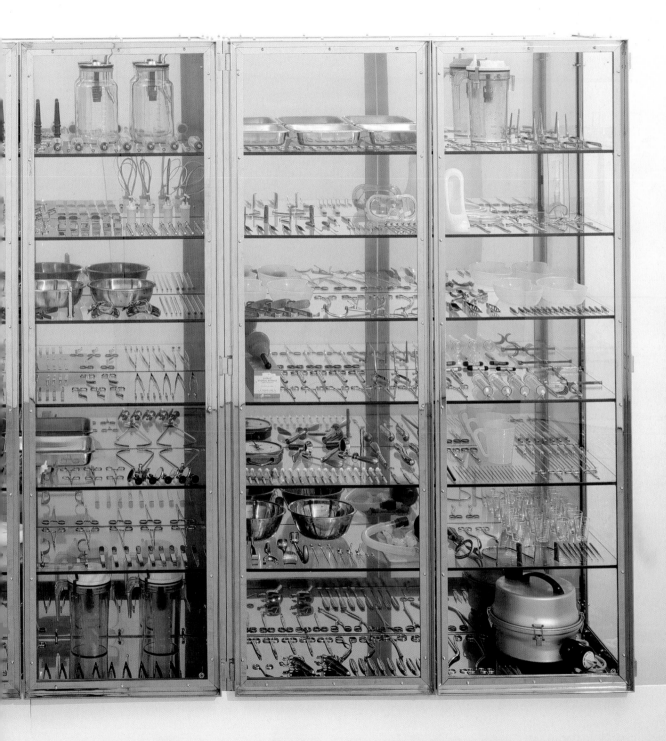

schiedliche Weise Richard Hamilton, Rachel Whiteread, Richard Wilson, Richard Wentworth und Jane und Louise Wilson. Mit seinen vielfältigen und intensiv verfolgten Interessen (von Wissenschaft und Technik bis Konsumkritik und Werbung, von Produktdesign, Typographie und seiner Auseinandersetzung mit dem Werk von Duchamp bis zu Politik und Macht) ist **Richard Hamilton** vom Vorläufer des British Pop, dessen Werk nichts von seiner herausfordernden Frische verloren hat, zu einem der beeindruckendsten, vielseitigsten und einflussreichsten Vertreter der britischen Kunst des zwanzigsten Jahrhunderts geworden.

Hamiltons mehrmonatiger Berlinaufenthalt 1974 gipfelte in einer großen Einzelausstellung in der Nationalgalerie. Während er in Berlin lebte, führte er seine Beschäftigung mit dem häuslichen Intérieur in einer Reihe von Arbeiten fort, die auf Aufnahmen in René Blocks Wohnung basieren (BERLIN INTERIORS). Dieses Thema begann 1956 mit seiner Collage JUST WHAT IS IT THAT MAKES TODAY'S HOMES SO DIFFERENT, SO APPEALING? (WAS MACHT HEUTIGE WOHNUNGEN EIGENTLICH SO ANDERS, SO REIZVOLL?), die in seinem Werk eine Schlüsselstellung einnimmt. Hamiltons Talent, sich selbst ständig neu zu

erfinden, auch heute noch im Alter von 79, wurde ganz besonders offenkundig bei der Kasseler documenta 1997. Damals arbeitete er zusammen mit Ecke Bonk an dem höchst anspruchsvollen, technisch komplexen Werk THE TYPOSOPHIC PAVILION und zeigte außerdem seine eindrucksvolle Installation mit dem Titel SEVEN ROOMS (die erstmals 1995 in der Anthony d'Offay Gallery in London zu sehen war). Diese ehrgeizige, computergenerierte Photofusion des Innenraums seiner Londoner Galerie mit dem Innenraum seines Bauernhauses in Oxfordshire, die fast wie eine Art von metaphorischem Selbstbildnis erscheint, ist der Ausgangspunkt für sämtliche drei aktuellen Gemälde in DOUBLE VISION.

Während SEVEN ROOMS jedoch kontemplative, stilllebenartige Räume ohne jede menschliche Präsenz zeigten, setzt Hamilton hier die menschliche Gestalt als zentrales Motiv ein. Wie der Künstler selbst bei der Diskussion über die Printversion von THE PASSAGE OF THE BRIDE erläutert: „Als Teil eines Plans, die SEVEN ROOMS zu bevölkern, bot eine Freundin an, in dem Haus, aus dem die Räume stammen, Modell zu stehen. Kodak stellte wieder eine Kamera zur Verfügung, und ich machte viele Aufnahmen, die sofort auf dem Computerbildschirm betrachtet

I believe in miracles.

werden konnten. (...) An der Westwand des Korridors hängt eine lebensgroße Bleistiftzeichnung des unteren Teils von Marcel Duchamps GROSSEM GLAS. Weil die Zeichnung so hell war, dass sie auf dem Originalphoto nicht zu sehen war, habe ich ein Transparent von Duchamps Apparat in die Paintbox eingescannt, es in Perspektive gesetzt und als Ersatz für die unsichtbare Zeichnung in die Leerstelle eingefügt. (...) Auf einer der Digitalaufnahmen ist das Modell beim Lesen eines Briefes am Fenster zu sehen. Weil die Gestalt zu weit entfernt war, rückte ich sie näher und stellte dann eine seitenverkehrte Kopie ins Bild. (...) Wenn man die Reflexion des Akts im Kontext zu Duchamp betrachtete, erschien die wiedergespiegelte Gestalt überflüssig." [1]

Mit ihrem Bezug auf Broodthaers im Titel basieren die Badezimmerbilder (FIG. 1 und FIG. 2) auf einem ähnlich komplexen Verfahren und einer Schichttechnik unter Beteiligung von Photographie (diesmal ist das Modell seine Frau, die Künstlerin Rita Donagh), Computermanipulation und schließlich der Wiedergabe des Bildes in Farbe und auf Leinwand.

Der Begriff der Interiorität ist fundamentaler Bestandteil von **Rachel Whiteread**s Arbeiten. Ausgehend von gewöhnlichen Alltagsgegenständen – einem Bett, einem Schrank, sogar einer Wasserflasche – für ihre mimetischen und doch kraftvoll transformierenden Abgüsse erforscht sie nicht nur unsere häuslichen Innenräume im Allgemeinen, sondern auch die inneren Leerstellen der Gegenstände, die diese Räume enthalten. Durch die Verwendung transparenter oder undurchsichtiger Materialien – wie Gips, Kautschuk oder Polyesterharz – zur Definition der Hohlräume besitzen die Skulpturen eine gleichermaßen vertraute wie gespenstische Erscheinung. In dieser Materialisierung von Raum, von Leere, von der gleichzeitigen Abwesenheit und Anwesenheit eines Gegenstands artikuliert sich der Kern von Whitereads Bestreben. Die Erinnerung an die Vergangenheit ist in jedem Werk hermetisch verschlossen und verkörperlicht Begriffe wie Sterblichkeit und *memento mori*. Interessant ist, dass Hirst und Whiteread, in Bekanntheitsgrad, Alter und Freundschaft miteinander verbunden, sich beide mit einem ähnlichen Thema auseinandersetzen, aber ganz gegensätzliche Stimmungen und Ausdrucksmittel benutzen. Ein Gefühl von Verlorenheit durchzieht ihr jeweiliges Werk, doch während Hirst Wut, Schrecken und Erschütterung bekundet, ent-

scheidet Whiteread sich für Melancholie, Stille und Kargheit.

Whiteread kam 1992 nach Berlin und blieb anderthalb Jahre. Es war eine außerordentlich produktive und inspirierende Zeit. Für eine Künstlerin, die das Thema Erinnerung mit so poetischer Intensität verfolgt, bot die Stadt Berlin eine gute Basis und reichlich Hintergrund für eigene Recherchen. Wie Whiteread bei mehreren Gelegenheiten anmerkte, hätte sie sich nie zugetraut, 1996 die angesehene, aber höchst einschüchternde Einladung nach Wien anzunehmen, um für einen Platz im Zentrum (den Judenplatz) ein Holocaust-Denkmal zu entwerfen, wenn sie nicht die Erfahrung gehabt hätte, in einer so geschichtsträchtigen Stadt wie Berlin gelebt und gearbeitet zu haben. Im Rahmen ihrer Recherchen zur Architektur von Krieg und Tod schuf Whiteread eine beachtliche Reihe von Skulpturen und Zeichnungen. Zu den wichtigsten (und für die Künstlerin persönlich bedeutungsvollsten) Werken, die in jener Zeit entstanden sind, gehören UNTITLED (CONCAVE AND CONVEX BEDS) (1992), zwei korrespondierende Matratzen-Abgüsse, die wie zusammengekrümmte, sich am Boden windende Körper wirken.

Für DOUBLE VISION hat Whiteread das gespenstische Echo eines Raumes geschaffen, mit Referenzen zu Bücherregalen, Tischen, Fußboden und Lichtschaltern. UNTITLED (STORIES), 1998, entstand zusammen mit weiteren Buch-und-Bibliothek-Skulpturen aus der Situation bedrückender Verzögerungen im Umfeld des Wiener Denkmals. Die drei waagerechten, zart abgestuften Pastellstreifen – Spuren der etwas grelleren Farbtöne auf den Taschenbüchern, von denen die Abgüsse stammen – rufen uns wieder in Erinnerung, dass Whiteread ursprünglich von der Malerei herkommt, und machen das Werk zu einer ihrer poetischsten Arbeiten. Formal gesehen erinnert der Kubus von UNTITLED (SIX SPACES), 1994, an die Sprache des Minimalismus sowie an die traditionelle Form eines Mausoleums. Seine verführerische Leuchtkraft wird weiter vervielfältigt in dem großartigen UNTITLED (ONE HUNDRED SPACES), 1995. UNTITLED (CAST CORRIDOR), aus Gusseisen hergestellt und dann mit Patina versehen, gehört zu Whitereads neuesten Arbeiten. Hier treten die Bezüge zum Minimalismus, vor allem zum Werk von Carl Andre, besonders stark hervor. Doch während Andres Bodenfliesen die makellose Oberfläche von Massenproduktion besitzen und das Allge-

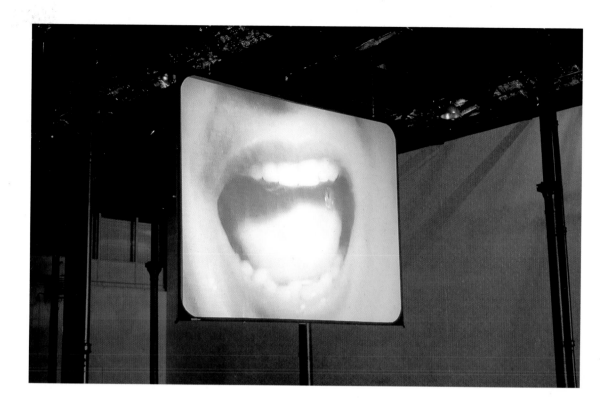

meine ansprechen, ist Whitereads sorgfältig von Hand gefertigter Korridor durchdrungen von Geschichte und dem Partikularen. Mit seiner sinnlichen und unregelmäßigen Oberfläche (die die Schritte der Besucher mit der Zeit weiter verändern werden), hat Whiteread einen Ort der Erinnerung geschaffen, einen diskreten Abdruck der Gegenwärtigkeit von Vergangenheit.

Die Verwendung von Alltagsgegenständen als Auslöser kollektiver Erinnerung und persönlicher Geschichte ist eine Trajektorie, die Whitereads Werk mit dem von Richard Wentworth verbindet. Wentworth, der Entscheidendes und Bahnbrechendes geleistet hat in seiner Rolle sowohl als Künstler wie als Lehrer (am Londoner Goldsmith College, der Wiege jener Generation der heute gefeierten jungen britischen Künstlerinnen und Künstler), trat Ende der siebziger Jahre erstmals mit einigen anderen britischen Bildhauern in Erscheinung, die sich in ihren Werken vornehmlich mit Alltagsgegenständen auseinandersetzten. Wentworths bildhauerisches Schaffen war immer geprägt von der Verwendung des einfachen, ja archetypischen „Dings". Hauptsächlich aus dem Bereich von Heim und Garten stammend, beziehen sich

seine Gegenstände oft auf uralte Formen. Wie Whiteread legt auch Wentworth Wert darauf, dass der Gegenstand gebraucht und häufig benutzt ist, Spuren von Abnutzung trägt und sich dadurch unser Verhältnis zu ihm manifestiert. Während der Künstler die Gegenstände selten bearbeitet, gelingt es ihm, einen radikalen Wandel in unserer Wahrnehmung ihrer Alltäglichkeit zu bewirken, indem er sie in faszinierende visuelle Rätsel umfunktioniert.

Wentworths Skulpturen verströmen etwas Spielerisches, einen gewissen Zauber und respektlosen Humor. Für seine Ausstellung TRAVELLING WITHOUT A MAP, die 1994 am Ende seines einjährigen Aufenthaltes in den Berliner Kunstwerken stattfand, schuf er eine seiner visuell faszinierendsten und gleichzeitig surreal geistreichsten Installationen: einen Wald aus unterschiedlich geformten und gefärbten Holzpfählen, die durch eine Vielzahl von „Requisiten" von unten (Bücher) und von oben (Teller) im Gleichgewicht gehalten schienen. Dass die Besucher, während sie sich zwischen den zahlreichen Pfählen durchlavierten, Schutzhelme tragen mussten, steigerte noch den Eindruck von Gefahr und Willkür der Installation. Dieses Gefühl wurde auch dadurch verstärkt,

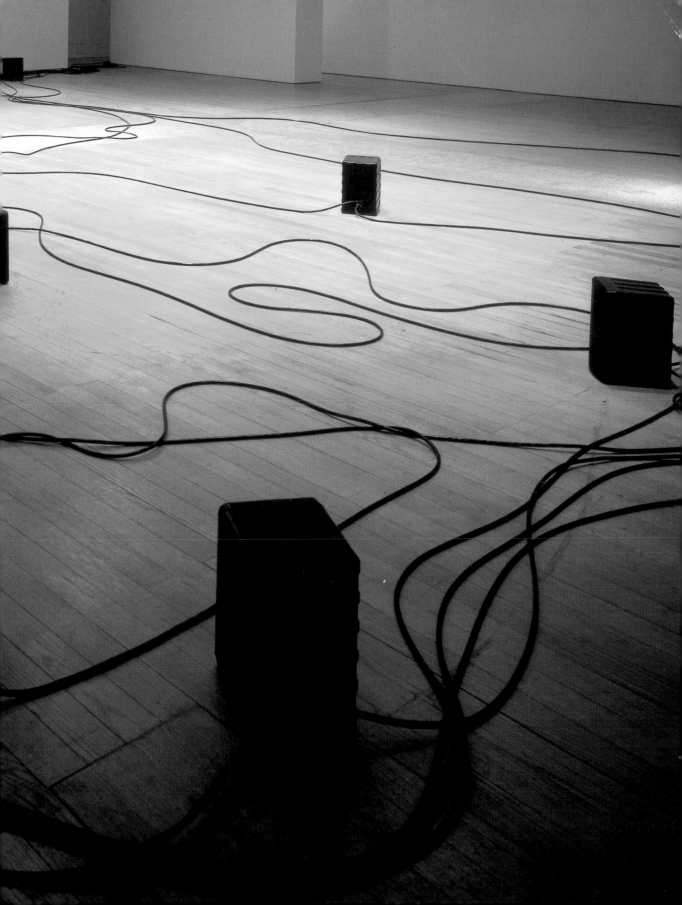

BERLIN INTERIOR, 1979
Photogravure, engraving,
etching, roulette, aquatint
and burnishing (Ed. 100)
49.7 x 69. 5 cm (image);
56. 3 x 76 cm (sheet)

dass man unweigerlich die klassische Zirkusnummer mit den wirbelnden Tellern auf schwankenden Stäben assoziierte (nur hatte Wentworth die Teller hier umgedreht ...).

Teller sind natürlich ein altes Lieblingsrequisit im Wentworthschen Repertoire. Ihre Zerbrechlichkeit, ihre unterschiedlichen Formen, besonderen lokalen Muster und volkstümlichen Farbstellungen sind für Wentworth ebenso wichtig wie ihre eigentliche alltägliche Funktion. Einem Zauberkünstler gleich verwandelt er sie einmal in hoch aufgetürmte Wolken (CUMULUS, 1991), dann in eine wogende, sich der Schwerkraft widersetzende Welle (FLIGHT, 1999) oder in eine Landschaft, das hier gezeigte SPREAD (1997). Der neobarocke Raum scheint die perfekte Folie für Wentworths geschicktes Spiel mit Erinnerung und Geschichte.

Wentworth ist der Inbegriff des städtischen Flaneurs, ein Chronist unserer menschlichen Verhaltenskodizes (besonders in ihren unterschiedlichen kulturellen Erscheinungsformen), unserer seltsamen Art, Dinge zu tun und praktische, wenngleich eigenwillige Lösungen zu finden. Seine Photoserie MAKING DO & GETTING BY zeigt seinen wachen Blick für die global verbindlichen Absurditäten des Lebens, für die Zufälle und Paradoxien. Diese Bilder sind außerordentlich unterhaltsam wie auch merkwürdig tröstlich in ihrer schwärmerisch-närrischen, allzu menschlichen Aussage. Während seines Aufenthalts in Deutschland hat Wentworth diese Serie mit dem Buch Berlin – 117 LANDMARKS / MARKSTEINE erweitert, wieder ein Kaleidoskop gut beobachteter, allzu vertrauter Tautologien und bizarrer deutscher Eigenarten, die gleichermaßen peinliche, liebenswerte und allgemeingültige Bildanekdoten erzählen.

Das Motiv des Innenraums setzt sich mit **Jane und Louise Wilson**s großformatigen Photo- und Video-Installationen fort. Sie erforschen spezifische Orte der Macht anhand der Anatomie ihrer Architektur, indem sie Form und Funktion mit der psychologischen „Aura" der Gebäude verknüpfen. Ihr ganzes Werk ist von einer merkwürdigen, an Hitchcock erinnernden Atmosphäre durchdrungen und ruft ein Gefühl von Ängstlichkeit vor oder Schock nach einem unbestimmten Gewaltakt hervor. Die Wilsons, die seit 1989 zusammenarbeiten, teilen mit Douglas Gordon das Interesse an der psychologischen Dimension und dem Wesen von Wahrnehmung, während die Faszination für das Unheimliche sie mit Mat Collishaw verbindet.

THE PASSAGE OF THE BRIDE,
1998-99
painting, oil on cibachrome
on canvas; 102 x 127 cm
Courtesy Richard Hamilton

Ihr DAAD-Stipendium in Hannover und Berlin führte zur Realisation ihres bisher vielleicht berühmtesten Films: Stasi City (1997) – ein Wendepunkt in ihrer Laufbahn. Gedreht im ehemaligen Gefängnis und Hauptquartier der ostdeutschen Geheimpolizei in Hohenschönhausen, war es der erste Film in einer Serie von komplexen Videoprojektionen über mehrere Leinwände, die sich mit dem Zusammenspiel zwischen Individuum und Gesellschaft und Überwachungsmechanismen auseinandersetzen. Nachdem sie bis dahin private, anonyme Drehorte wie verlassene Wohnungen oder schäbige Hotelzimmer gewählt hatten, verlagerten sie mit Stasi City die geheimnisvolle und unheimliche Atmosphäre ihrer Innenräume in den öffentlichen Bereich. „In Berlin wurde uns besonders das Verhältnis zwischen historischer Architektur und Kaltem Krieg bewusst. Die politischen Unterschiede zwischen Ost- und West-Deutschland konzentrierten sich auf die Bedeutungsträchtigkeit von Gebäuden, auf das, was bestimmte Orte darstellten."[2]

In Star City (2000), ihrem neuesten Film – zusammen mit Gamma (1999) und Parliament (1999) die vierte Video-Installation, die sich mit Orten der Macht befasst – werden wir ins Innere eines russischen Raumfahrttrai-

ningszentrums in der Nähe von Moskau geführt. Wieder wird der Betrachter auf eine gleichsam hypnotisierende Bilderreise mitgenommen, diesmal durch eine während der Sowjetzeit mehr oder weniger verborgene Stadt, die besonders seit Beginn der Zusammenarbeit zwischen amerikanischen und russischen Raumfahrtbehörden nun aber zugänglicher geworden ist. Weiterhin bestehende Differenzen zwischen den beiden Supermächten werden in der Eröffnungsszene des Films vorsichtig angedeutet, die die russischen und amerikanischen Unterkünfte vor Ort miteinander kontrastiert. Während sich die Kamera hineinbewegt, gewinnen wir einen Einblick in entvölkerte, geheime Räume und Durchgänge und gelangen schließlich in ein ehemals zukunftsweisendes Speziallabor für Hydrotechnik, in dem Schwerelosigkeit simuliert wird – an einen Ort, der nicht nur strengen Drill und Forschertätigkeit signalisiert, sondern auch nationalen Ehrgeiz und den utopischen Traum von der Eroberung des Weltraums. Innenräume mit gespenstisch widerhallender Leere und einer Atmosphäre düsterer Verlassenheit werden auf vier Leinwände projiziert. Der so entstehende stereoskopische Effekt umgibt den Betrachter mit einer klaustrophobischen und sinnesverwirrenden Vision von Dystopie.

BATHROOM FIG. 1, 1999
painting, oil on cibachrome
on canvas; 50 x 50 cm
Courtesy Rita Donagh

BATHROOM FIG. 2, 1999/2000
painting, oil on cibachrome
on canvas; 100 x 100 cm
Courtesy Richard Hamilton

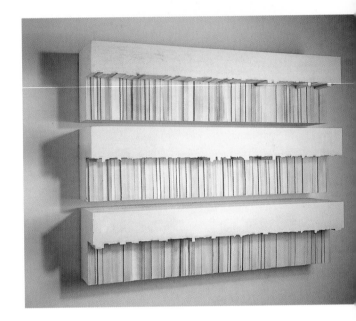

Untitled (24 switches), 1998
aluminium
26.3 x 20.3 x 6 cm
Private Collection

Untitled (Stories), 1998
polystyrene and plaster
99 x 120 x 26 cm
Private Collection

Die Beschäftigung mit architektonischen Räumen und deren historischer, politischer und gesellschaftlicher Bedeutung setzt sich in dieser Ausstellung mit Filmen von Victor Burgin und Tacita Dean sowie Photoarbeiten von Stephen Willats und Willie Doherty fort, die alle im oberen Stockwerk zu sehen sind. **Victor Burgin** wurde in den siebziger Jahren durch seine Schwarzweißphoto-Text-Arbeiten bekannt, in denen sich immer wieder auftauchende Themen wie Voyeurismus, Überwachung, Stadt und Entfremdung mit ihren Bezügen zu klassischen Filmtraditionen verbinden. Während seiner Zeit in Berlin entstand 1978 die Photoserie aus acht Diptychen mit dem Titel Zoo 78, eine „Dramatisierung bestimmter Fragestellungen der sexualpolitischen Theorie innerhalb eines Gebiets (Berlin), dessen physische, politische und historische Struktur zur Vorführung dieser Fragestellungen in einzigartiger Weise ausgestattet ist"[3].

In Double Vision ist Victor Burgin mit Nietzsche's Paris (1999) vertreten, einer aufwendigen Videoprojektion, die auf die schicksalhafte historische Begegnung zwischen Friedrich Nietzsche, Lou Andreas Salomé und Paul Rée im Jahre 1882 in Leipzig Bezug nimmt. Sie hatten geplant, ein intellektuelles Dreiecksverhältnis einzu-

gehen und in Paris unter ein Dach zu ziehen. Nachdem man sich in Leipzig getroffen hatte, um letzte Absprachen zu treffen, sieht Nietzsche sich plötzlich von den anderen beiden im Stich gelassen und nimmt fälschlicherweise an, dass sie nach Paris geflohen sind. Dieser dramatische Ablauf der Geschichte wird im Film jedoch vollständig ausgeklammert, ebenso jedwede Beschreibung von Leipzig. Stattdessen begegnen wir computermanipulierten, menschenleeren Aufnahmen von der Pariser Bibliothèque Nationale. Burgin schreibt über das gewählte Bild folgendermaßen: „Obwohl sie in bitterer Entfremdung endete, hatte die kurze Beziehung zwischen Nietzsche und Salomé während der drei Augustwochen, die sie zusammen im Wald von Tautenberg mit Diskussionen über Philosophie verbrachten, eine Phase idyllischer Intimität durchlaufen. Die historische Assoziation zwischen Wäldern, Gärten und Bildung wird von Dominique Pérrault in der kürzlich fertig gestellten Bibliothèque Nationale de France weidlich ausgenutzt. Pérraults versunkener Waldgarten in der Mitte des Gebäudes wurde von einem Kritiker passend beschrieben als ‚unberührbares Paradies' zu dem Forscher und Öffentlichkeit keinen Zutritt haben. Im Gedenken an

UNTITLED (SIX SPACES), 1996
resin
51 x 38 x 38 cm each
Courtesy Arts Council Collection,
Hayward Gallery, London

Nietzsches paradiesische Zeit mit der unerreichbaren Lou taucht eben dieser Pariser Ort in der Arbeit auf."[4]

Im Film werden Segmente jener kühlen Architektur mit kurzen Blicken auf eine im Stil des neunzehnten Jahrhunderts gekleideten Frau zusammengeschnitten, die in einem üppigen grünen Park oder Wald reglos auf einer Bank sitzt. Dieser Zusammenprall von unterschiedlichen zeitlichen Momenten wird durch die alternierende Verwendung von Schwarzweiß für eine Sequenz und Farbe für die andere unterstrichen. Die Untermalung mit Barockmusikfragmenten (aus Händels ALCINA am Anfang und seiner ARIODANTE gegen Ende der Filmschleife) ist besonders geschickt gewählt, da die architektonische Qualität der Musik mit den Gebäude-Aufnahmen genau synchron geht und beide Opernfragmente außerdem Dreiecksbeziehungen zum Thema haben. Burgin treibt die Dichotomien aber noch weiter: Die friedliche Ruhe von Bildern und Musik steht im Kontrast zur emotionalen Aufgewühltheit der implizierten Personen. Der Rationalismus der modernen Architektur wird konterkariert vom Irrationalismus der in Käfige gesperrten Bäume, die als Metapher für gescheiterte utopische Konzepte zu fungieren scheinen.[5]

NIETZSCHE'S PARIS gehört zu einer Reihe von neueren Videoarbeiten, die durch Verwendung von Opernfragmenten, in Originalsprache gesprochenem Text und historischen Konnotationen über Text, Musik und Kostüm miteinander verbunden sind (LOVE LETTERS, 1997; LICHTUNG, 1998-99; ANOTHER CASE HISTORY, 1999; WATERGATE, 2000; ELECTIVE AFFINITIES, 2001).

Das Thema der gescheiterten Utopie, ausgedrückt durch ein architektonisches Wahrzeichen, nimmt auch Tacita Deans neuester Film FERNSEHTURM auf. Aufgenommen an einem perfekten Sommerabend letztes Jahr in dem drehbaren Restaurant, das sich hoch über den Straßen von Berlin erhebt, zeichnet er von Sonnenuntergang bis Einbruch der Dunkelheit vierundvierzig Minuten des Lebens und Treibens darin auf. Der Fernsehturm auf dem Alexanderplatz, im Herzen der ehemaligen ostdeutschen Hauptstadt gelegen und eine der berühmtesten Sehenswürdigkeiten der Stadt, ist wohl das mächtigste Symbol der nationalen Identität der früheren DDR, eine bleibende Mahnung an ihre Hoffnungen und Ambitionen. Gleichzeitig deutet der Turm auf die immer noch bestehenden Unterschiede zwischen den beiden Teilen

der Stadt: für Ostdeutsche eine der beliebtesten Touristenattraktionen, wird er von Leuten aus dem Westen weitgehend ignoriert. Man mag es auch als ein weiteres Zeichen des Wandels und des Ost-West-Kontrasts sehen, dass die Geschwindigkeit, mit der sich das Restaurant dreht, seit der Vereinigung verdoppelt wurde. Früher dauerte eine komplette Umdrehung gemächliche sechzig Minuten, jetzt sind es nunmehr dreißig.

Ursprünglich ungewiss darüber, ob es einer Ausländerin, die erst seit kurzem in Deutschland war, überhaupt zustand, einen Film über ein mit kultureller und politischer Bedeutung so befrachtetes Bauwerk zu machen, war Dean bald völlig von der idealen Eignung des Turmes für ihre Arbeit in Bann gezogen. Für sie ist FERNSEHTURM die konzeptuell logische Erweiterung nach einer Reihe von Filmen, die sich mit architektonischen Anachronismen oder Metaphern für zunichte gemachte Hoffnungen und aussichtslose Sehnsüchte befassen, wie etwa BUBBLEHOUSE (1999) oder SOUND MIRRORS (1999). In DISAPPEARANCE AT SEA (1996), vielleicht ihrem betörendsten Werk, richtet sie den Blick nicht nur auf ein weiteres nostalgisches Bauwerk, einen Leuchtturm, sondern wählt auch den gleichen dezidiert gefühlsträchtigen

Augenblick, wenn der Tag in die Nacht übergeht. Über den Fernsehturm schrieb die Künstlerin kürzlich in einem Zeitungsartikel: „Erbaut zu einer Zeit, als wir an die Raumfahrt glaubten, wirkt er futuristisch und kühn, und verharrt doch im Dekor und Optimismus der sechziger Jahre. Die sich im Raum drehende Sphäre symbolisiert für uns die Zukunft immer noch am besten und ist doch Stilelement aus einer anderen, vergangenen Zeit."[6]

Am meisten fasziniert an dieser Arbeit der sich ständig verändernde Eindruck von Atmosphäre, Licht, Klang und Raum im Inneren des Restaurants. Das konstante Element in diesem Gewebe sich verschiebender Koordinaten ist das majestätische Band von schrägen Fensterrahmen, das gleichzeitig wie ein Echo des Abfolgerhythmus eines Filmstreifens fungiert, und die sichere Gewandtheit der schwarzweiß gekleideten Kellner alten Stils. Wir werden durch einen kompletten Zyklus der abendlichen Routine des Restaurants geführt, das erst leer, dann voll und wieder leer ist, von laut bis leise, hell bis dunkel, von unendlichen Ausblicken bei Tageslicht bis zur dunklen, nach innen gerichteten Stimmung des nächtlichen Raums. Trotz der Alltäglichkeit, ja Banalität des Cafébetriebs besitzt die Szenerie eine

26/27 UNTITLED (CONCAVE AND CONVEX BEDS), 1992
Rubber and neoprene
Two units: 40 x 100 x 196 cms and 34 x 100 x 196 cms
Courtesy Anthony d'Offay Gallery, London

hypnotische Wirkung, die sich in etwas ganz Universales übersetzt. Wenn ein Glas Wein von den Strahlen der untergehenden Sonne in ein glühend schillerndes Gefäß verwandelt wird, wenn die Szene ständig zwischen Schatten und Licht changiert, fängt Dean in den alltäglichen Freuden von Essen und Trinken ganz sublime Momente ein. Der Film wirkt wie die Zelebrierung der transformativen Kraft des Lichts, des Vergehens von Zeit, das sich mit jeder neuen Umdrehung des Restaurants innerhalb seiner Sphäre und des grenzenlosen Raums draußen manifestiert. Zusammen mit den spektakulären Lichtveränderungen wird FERNSEHTURM ein zum Planetenlauf paralleler Mikrokosmos.

Architektur als konstituierendes Element von Identität ist auch die Basis des einflussreichen künstlerischen Schaffens von Stephen Willats. Indem er direkt in die gesellschaftliche Struktur einer Stadt eintaucht, arbeitet er wie ein urbaner Anthropologe und stellt seine Kunst in enge Verbindung zu soziologischen Untersuchungen. Die Ergebnisse seiner Recherchen, Ausbeute zahlloser Photos und Interviews, werden als diagrammatische Photocollagen auf Schautafeln gezeigt.

Willats verankert seine vielseitigen Projekte in bestimmten gesellschaftlichen Gruppen. Seine „Feldforschungen" führt er meistens in modernen Sozialwohnsiedlungen, wie etwa Hochhausblocks, durch – ein weiterer utopischer Traum der sechziger und siebziger Jahre – sowohl in London wie auch in Mietshäusern in Berlin, Eindhoven oder New York.[7]

Willats konzentrierte seine Recherche in Berlin 1979-80 (und während eines erneuten Aufenthalts 1992) auf zwei Hauptzentren von Sozialwohnsiedlungen, das Märkische Viertel und die Gropiusstadt, und richtete dabei sein Augenmerk auf die Themen Isolation und Abhängigkeit. Zusätzlich wählte er eine Gartenparzelle und eine Boutique, um die Themen Flucht bzw. Passivität zu beleuchten. Nach ersten, oft komplizierten Versuchen der Kontaktaufnahme zu den Menschen, die an den jeweiligen Orten lebten oder arbeiteten, und nachdem er ihr Vertrauen zur Zusammenarbeit gewonnen hatte, begann Willats mit den Interviews: „Der nächste Schritt bestand darin, jeden Teilnehmer auf Band aufzunehmen (...) In der ursprünglichen Aufnahme stellte ich sehr einfache, beschreibende Fragen über die Umgebung und die Aktivitäten, die dort stattfanden (...) Dann ging ich in

UNTITLED (CAST CORRIDOR), 2000
cast iron (24 units); 1.5 x 226 x 405 cm
Courtesy Collection Robert R. Littman
and Sully Bonnelly

31 Travelling without a Map
Kunstwerke Berlin, 1994

einer weiteren Sitzung dazu über, die Umgebung, bestimmte Gegenstände darin und meine Gesprächspartner zu photographieren (...) Nachdem ich meinen ersten Satz Dokumentationsmaterial gesichtet hatte, formulierte ich für jeden Teilnehmer zehn Fragen aus, die sich direkt auf die verschiedenen Zielsetzungen jeder Arbeit richteten (...) Meine Dokumentationen erstreckten sich über einen durchschnittlichen Zeitraum von sechs Monaten und erforderten fünf oder sechs Besuche. Das Ergebnis war, dass ich alle Teilnehmer recht gut kennen lernte und sie sich auch an mich gewöhnten und viel zugänglicher und hilfsbereiter bei der Durchführung der Dokumentation wurden, indem sie mir sagten, was ich fotografieren sollte und was ihrer Meinung nach an ihrem Leben für meine ‚Arbeit' wichtig war (...). Die Entscheidung, welche Bezüge im [endgültigen] Werk verwendet werden sollten, lag zwar bei mir, zusammen mit den Vorschlägen meines Assistenten, doch hatten die Teilnehmer das letzte Wort. (...) Die Bandbreite an Reaktionen variiert beträchtlich: Der Bewohner des Hochhausblocks fand meine Anmerkungen zu seinem Leben zu negativ und änderte viele Zitate positiv um, während der Hausmeister (im Märkischen Viertel) alles so akzep-

tierte, wie es war und meinte: ‚So ist das Leben, genauso ist es'."[8]

Mit seinem partizipatorisch ausgerichteten Arbeitsmodell, das er Mitte der sechziger Jahre entwickelte, wurde Willats zum Pionier einer demokratischen Kunstform, die die Entstehung eines Werks als von der Interaktion zwischen Menschen abhängigen Prozess begreift. Der Künstler nicht als Produzent autonomer Objekte, sondern als Katalysator, der dem Alltäglichen und Nebensächlichen Vorrang einräumt, ist zum bedeutenden Konzept in der Kunst der vergangenen zehn Jahre geworden.

Die Betonung scheinbar distanziert-nüchterner Methoden dokumentarischer Reportage lässt sich auch in den Videos und Photos von **Willie Doherty** beobachten. Wie bei Willats deuten Dohertys Bilder das Spezifische und Generelle, das Individuelle und Universale an. Was Dohertys einzigartige Stellung jedoch vor allem ausmacht, ist seine nordische Herkunft – daher die politische Perspektive, auf der sein Werk basiert. Seine Photos und Videoprojektionen wurden größtenteils in und um seine Heimatstadt Derry oder deren Umgebung aufge-

nommen – bzw. Londonderry, die alte, befestigte Stadt ist unter ihrem kolonialen Namen besser bekannt. Doherty deutet die andauernde Unlösbarkeit des irischen Konflikts zwar an, ergreift aber nie Partei, und diese nicht kritisierende, nicht idealisierende Haltung bewog Carolyn Christov Bakargiev, seine Arbeit als „meta-politisch" zu bezeichnen. Derry ist bekanntermaßen seit Jahrzehnten einer der Brennpunkte sektiererischer Gewalt: Hier fanden 1972 die berüchtigten Mordaktionen des Blutigen Sonntags statt.

Dohertys Bilder zeigen eine Vorliebe für den Nicht-Ort, das anonyme, von Verlassenheit und Vernachlässigung geprägte Niemandsland zwischen dem ländlichen und dem urbanen Raum. Dass er bisher sein ganzes Leben in einer so polarisierten und unruhigen Stadt wie Derry verbrachte, hat das Bewusstsein des Künstlers für die psychologische Wirkung von Grenzen und das klischeehafte Konstrukt der „Feind"- oder „Terrorist"-Identität geschärft. In SAME DIFFERENCE (1990), einer frühen Dia-Text-Installation zeigt er beispielsweise, wie Wahrnehmung durch Sprache und Unterstellung manipuliert werden kann. Es schien daher ganz besonders naheliegend, Willie Doherty in eine Stadt einzuladen, die über so viele

Jahre vom Zustand des Eingemauertseins und einem inhärenten Gefühl der Teilung geprägt war, damit er dort seine Recherchen zum Thema Kontextualisierung und Eingrenzung nationaler Identitäten fortführen konnte.

Seit Mitte der neunziger Jahre haben Dohertys Videoarbeiten und Farb-Cibachromes ein zunehmend konturloses Terrain erschlossen. Sie setzen sich weiter mit unterschwelligen Ängsten und Befürchtungen auseinander, zeigen die Ambiguität von Ort und Position jedoch ausgeprägter. Seine jüngste, hier gezeigte Arbeit, EXTRACTS FROM A FILE, ist eine Serie von 40 kleinformatigen Photos zugiger Treppenhäuser und vereinzelter, erleuchteter Fenster, aufgenommen in den nächtlichen Straßen Berlins. Nach den komplexen mehrfach Projektionen, die in den letzten Jahren entstanden sind, signalisiert EXTRACTS FROM A FILE eine rigorose formale Vereinfachung sowie die Rückkehr zu Dohertys ersten Schwarzweißphotos – die allerdings mit politisch aufgeladenen Texten überlagert und hinter Glasrahmen gestellt waren. Dieses Distanzierungsmittel fehlt hier, und die menschenleeren Nachtszenen sind so durchdrungen von dichter, samtiger Finsternis, dass jegliches Geschehen geisterhaft wirkt. Beim näheren Hinsehen

Berlin 1993

MAKING DO & GETTING BY, 1976-99
framed photographs
43.5 x 51 cm each
Courtesy Lisson Gallery, London

erweisen sie sich nicht als die harmlosen Visionen eines nächtlichen Spaziergängers, sondern entfalten eine rätselhaft emotionsgeladene Atmosphäre. Es entsteht der Eindruck von geheimer Überwachung, der psychologische Effekt ist Spannung, in düsteren Durchgängen lauert die Angst. Wie Tacita Dean hat es Doherty ja schon immer gereizt, die Grenzen zwischen Fakt und Fiktion, Reportage und Kunstgriff, Dokumentation und Rätsel zu verwischen.

Bezüge zu Architektur und häuslichen Innenräumen tauchen auch wieder im Werk von **Richard Wilson** auf, dessen gespaltene, auseinandergeschnittene und zerlegte neue Möbel-Skulpturen für DOUBLE VISION durch ständiges Umkehren von Innen und Außen enthüllen, was normalerweise verborgen bleibt. Wie Rachel Whiteread und Richard Wentworth wendet sich auch Wilson auf der Suche nach Inspiration dem Häuslichen oder „Heimelig-Vertrauten" zu. In seinen Interventionen werden Stühle und Aktenschränke, aber auch Schwimmbecken, Gartenschuppen oder Gewächshäuser aufgehängt, filetiert oder verkehrt und konfrontieren uns mit einer Erfahrung oder Ahnung von Risiko, Gefahr oder den Nachwirkungen von Gewalt.

Eine seiner bisher vielleicht spektakulärsten Arbeiten schuf Wilson letzthin für das Skulpturenprojekt um den Millennium Dome in London. Als Tribut an die Geschichte der einst pulsierenden Handelsschifffahrt auf der Themse zog er das mittlere „slice" (die Mittel„scheibe"), inklusive der Brücke, durch den Rumpf eines riesigen, 30 Jahre alten Flussbaggers, den er nicht weit vom Ufer so in die Themse stellte, dass die Fluten durch das freigelegte Skelett ein und aus strömten. Auf dem Scheitelpunkt von Land und Wasser, von Objekt und Architektur, Vergangenheit und Gegenwart gelegen, war SLICE OF REALITY gleichermaßen melancholisch und feierlich. Wie sein geistiger Vorgänger Gordon Matta-Clark, schneidet, sägt und bohrt Wilson in den Baukörper, um dessen Segmente danach auf sinnesverwirrende Weise neu anzuordnen. In seinem inzwischen legendären Werk 20:50 erlebt man die Umkehrung gewohnter Perzeptionsweisen fast halluzinatorisch: Literweise eingebrachtes Senkgrubenöl bildet eine glänzende schwarze Fläche von enormen Ausmaßen, in der sich die Decke makellos wiederspiegelt und jeden Versuch einer räumlichen Interpretation buchstäblich verkehrt. Den Besucher durch die Brechung gewohnter Wahrnehmungsmuster

Auguststraße

Eisenacher Straße

zu verwirren, ist das gemeinsame Ziel aller gewagten Installationen Wilsons.

Wilson ist da in seinem Element, wo er sich direkt in die architektonische Struktur eines Gebäudes eingreifen kann. Als die Serpentine Gallery ihn vor einem größeren Renovierungsvorhaben zu ihrer Abschlussausstellung einlud, bot die absolute Freiheit, mit dem Gebäude nach Belieben verfahren zu dürfen, das ideale Szenario. Seine dortige Ausstellung 1996 mit dem Titel JAMMING GEARS war fast ausschließlich um die Erwartung des bevorstehenden Zusammenbruchs konstruiert. Invasionen von Gabelstaplern und Bauhütten, in gefährlich schiefen Winkeln aufgestellt, als hätte ein Wirbelsturm durch die Gallerie gefegt, agierten als Vorboten der geplanten Renovierung. In brutal und respektlos wirkender Geste stach Wilson unzählige tiefe, kreisrunde Löcher in den Steinboden der Galerie, ja durch ganze Wände von intakten Bücherregalen und bohrte sogar die Decke bis zum Himmel durch, was das Gebäude zwar verletzlich machte, jedoch auch Blicke und Aussichten eröffnete, die unerwartete Verbindungen herstellten. Die zufällige Beobachtung einer solchen Kreisbohrung auf einer typischen Berliner Baustelle während seines DAAD-Stipendiums hatte Wilson zu diesem außergewöhnlichen Werk inspiriert.

Die intensive Beschäftigung mit Stofflichkeit, gepaart mit dem Vergnügen an deren Wandlungsfähigkeit und metaphorischer Deutungskraft, lässt sich auch im Werk von Vong Phaophanit entdecken. Geboren in Laos, ausgebildet in Frankreich, jedoch seit 1986 in Großbritannien lebend, begann Phaophanit ursprünglich mit Installationen aus Materialien, die an sein Heimatland erinnern – wie z.B. Reis, Bambus, Seide und Kautschuk. Diese organischen, mit vielfältigen historischen und wirtschaftlichen Assoziationen behafteten Substanzen kontrastierte er zuweilen mit (vorherrschend roten) Neonleuchtröhren. Manchmal, wie in NEON RICE FIELD in einer schlichten, geraden Linie, öfter aber zu laotischen Schriftzeichen geformt, ergänzt das Neon die verführerische Stofflichkeit der organischen Substanzen mit einem künstlichen Leuchten und der Idee von Sprache – einer Sprache allerdings, deren Bedeutung den meisten Betrachtern verborgen bleibt. Im leuchtenden Dunstschleier der Textarbeiten wird Kommunikation absichtsvoll vorenthalten.

STASI CITY, 1997
4 Laserdiscs in a 5 minute cycle
Installation view
Courtesy Lisson Gallery, London

STASI CITY, 1997
C-type print on aluminium
270 x 125 cm
Courtesy Lisson Gallery, London

Die Unlesbarkeit ist gelegentlich noch gesteigert, wenn Hunderte von blauen Neonwörtern in einem langen, unter dem Galerieboden konstruierten Graben willkürlich übereinander gehäuft werden (AZURE BLUE BODY, 1994) oder wenn in einer neueren unbetitelten Wand-Installation fünf Lagen laotischer Schriftzeichen voreinander gesetzt werden. Licht ist in Phaophanits Arbeiten ein zentrales Merkmal: Es überflutet die Betrachter und verwandelt sie in flirrende chromatische Mitspieler (ähnlich wie bei Douglas Gordons SOMETHING BETWEEN MY MOUTH AND YOUR EAR, wo der Zuschauer ganz in blaues Licht getaucht wird, die Farbe der Erinnerung).

Seit Phaophanits Berlinaufenthalt lässt sich eine markante Veränderung und Zäsur in seinem Werk feststellen. Der Wechsel von organischen hin zu synthetischen Materialien manifestierte sich auf eindrucksvolle Weise in ATOPIA, seiner Ausstellung an zwei Orten, die 1997 in Berlin gezeigt wurde. In einer Dach-Installation bohrten sich Tausende von weißen Taubenstacheln – die allgegenwärtige und ziemlich brutale Vogelabwehr auf vielen öffentlichen Gebäuden – in den Himmel und verwandelten eine ganz gewöhnliche, leere Dachfläche in einen rätselhaften, gefährlich wirkenden weißen Zauber-

teppich, der zum Betreten einlud und es gleichzeitig verwehrte. Während seiner Zeit in Deutschland begann Phaophanit mit synthetischem Gummi zu experimentieren. In der daadgalerie stellte er lange Reihen von Metallregalen auf, die mit drei Tonnen Polybutadein beladen waren, einem langsam und obszön heruntertriefenden Material, bei dessen Anblick einem grotesk mutierende oder verwesende Kreaturen in den Sinn kamen. Die Assoziation von lebenden, wenngleich fremdartigen Organismen, von der Züchtung einer bedrohlichen, noch unbekannten Spezies, hat etwas Unheimliches und Überwältigendes. Für DOUBLE VISION erweitert Phaophanit diese Idee: Er konstruiert hier einen gewaltigen, mit schaurigen, triefenden Gummiklumpen beladenen Turm, um den die Besucher sich auf dem beengten Raum der Installation vorsichtig herummanövrieren müssen. Das klaustrophobische Gefühl und der Kunstgriff, dem Betrachter mit einer Art Barriere den Weg zu verstellen, tauchen in seinem Werk immer wieder auf (ASH AND SILK WALL, IN THE SHADOW OF WORDS, LITTERAE LUCENTES, WHAT FALLS TO THE GROUND BUT CAN'T BE EATEN?). In den meisten Fällen lassen sich Phaophanits Barrieren allerdings durchschreiten oder überqueren, ja erfordern es sogar.

Skarfaundry, 2000
C-print on aluminium
180 x 180 cm
Courtesy Lisson Gallery, London

38/39 Star City, 2000
four screen video installation
screens 410 x 310 cm each
Courtesy Lisson Gallery, London,
and 303 Gallery, New York

Für **Mat Collishaw** besitzt das Unheimliche und Bizarre ebenfalls eine starke Anziehungskraft. Seine Serie Infectious Flowers führt eine ähnliche Dualität von Schönheit und Krankheit, Anziehung und Abscheu vor wie Phaophanits metamorphisierende Gummiskulpturen. Collishaws in Lichtboxen gestellte Bilder zeigen Nahaufnahmen von prächtigen Blumen in voller Blüte. Auf den zweiten Blick offenbart sich jedoch ihre Bedrohlichkeit: In digitaler Verschmelzung mit Abbildungen verschiedener Hautkrankheiten entarten die Blumen zu abscheulichen, giftigen Gebilden. Diese Zersetzung von Vollkommenheit und Unschuld setzt Collishaw als Strategie in seinem photographischen Werk häufig ein: Bilder von exotischen Blumen, schlafenden jungen Mädchen oder nackten Knaben sind durchtränkt vom Flair des Verdorbenen – der Schlaf der Mädchen entpuppt sich als von Betäubungsmitteln hervorgerufen, rings um die Knaben herrscht urbaner Verfall und Zerstörung.

Collishaws Werk thematisiert Begriffe wie Sexualität, Gewalt und Voyeurismus sowie Probleme der heutigen Zeit und Fragen unserer persönlichen Moral. Sein außerordentlich vielfältiges Schaffen kombiniert High-Tech und Low-Tech, Photographie, Videoprojektion und

Installation. Ungewöhnlicherweise für einen Künstler seiner Generation stammt sein historisches Quellenmaterial oft aus dem 19. Jahrhundert. Dies reflektiert sich in den zahlreichen viktorianischen Requisiten, die er in seinen Video-Installationen verwendet, sowie in der Wahl seiner Themen (Baron von Gloedens Aufnahmen inspirierten ihn zu seiner Ideal Boys-Serie, Wright of Derbys An Experiment on a Bird in the Air Pump zu seiner Video-Skulptur Antique).

Sein Berlinjahr war Inspiration zur Entwicklung von Burnt Almonds, seine bisher einzige Arbeit, die sich auf einen spezifischen Moment der Geschichte bezieht. Diese Serie dreidimensionaler, bikonvexer Photographien, setzt den Selbstmord von Nazigrößen im Augenblick der Niederlage 1945 in finsteren Bunkern nach einer Orgie mit Sex, Alkohol und Drogen dramatisch in Szene. Statt der nüchternen Bebilderung historischer Tatsachen führt uns der Künstler ein opernhaftes, jämmerliches Porträt vom Ende des Dritten Reiches vor.

Für Double Vision hat Collishaw ein neues Werk geschaffen, basierend auf Videomaterial, das er während seines Berlinaufenthalts im dortigen Zoo aufgenommen hat. Shangri La ist die Vision vom irdischen

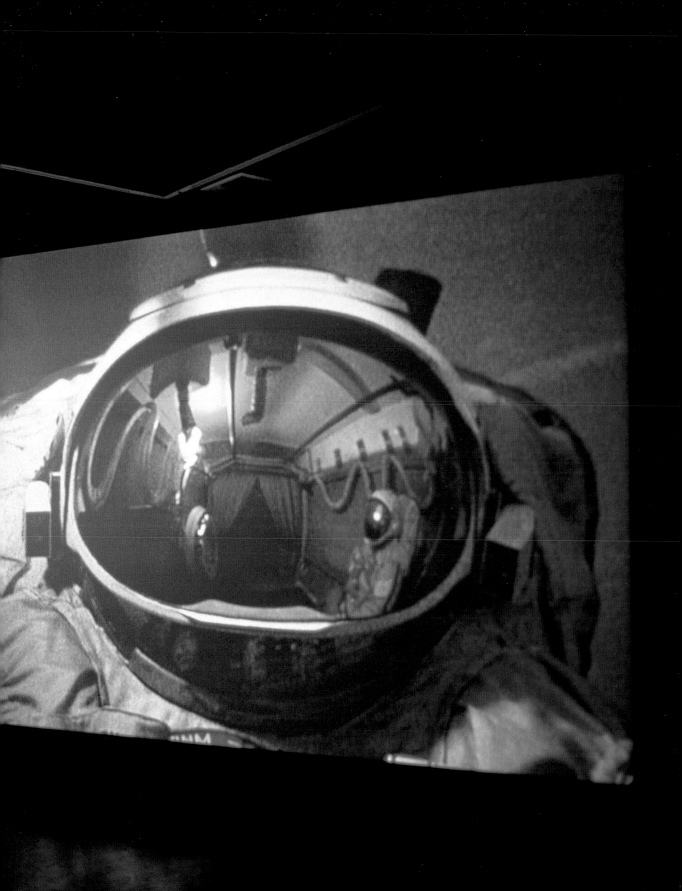

'A wide moat surrounds her and prevents any approach. The pedestal upon which she is posed is connected to a chair by a means of which the person in the chair could cause the pedestal to turn in such a manner that the object of his admiration could be viewed from every angle'. Sade reports that Valmont was free to examine Eugénie for half an hour: '...he is beside himself ...the constantly moving cord offfers him an endless succession of new angles...to which shall he sacrifice himself?'

Paradies und Weltfrieden, wo Menschen aller ethnischen Zugehörigkeiten sich in jeweiliger Nationaltracht zu einem idyllischen Picknick im Grünen versammeln. Man könnte darin das utopische und idealistische Gegenstück zu den Arbeiten Collishaws sehen, die sich mit der hoffnungslosen Lage von Menschen am Rand der Gesellschaft auseinandersetzen – mit Obdachlosen und Prostituierten. Allerdings weit davon entfernt, einfacher Chronist des modernen Lebens zu sein, inszeniert Collishaw seine Videos im Reich des Magischen: Der Obdachlose sieht sich plötzlich in eine Schneekugel, die Prostituierte mitten auf die künstliche Lilie in einem Teich projiziert, und das utopische Picknick von SHANGRI LA findet, wie sich herausstellt, in einem altmodischen, baufälligen Zelt statt. Von diesem Dualismus, der Gegenüberstellung von Unschuld und Erfahrung, Idylle und Großstadtdschungel, Romantik und Dekadenz, Gut und Böse, Realität und Imagination, lebt Collishaws gesamtes Werk.

Obwohl er erst 32 ist, zeigt **Steve McQueen** in seinen Filmen eine bemerkenswert sichere Handhabung dieses Mediums. Stark beeinflusst von der Filmgeschichte, und dabei insbesondere von ausländischen Filmen, hat Steve McQueen eine faszinierende Bildersprache und einen höchst anspruchsvollen, individuellen Stil entwickelt. Wie Jane und Louise Wilson tritt er in seinen Filmen auch selbst auf, ohne dass sie jedoch „von ihm" handeln. Mit Tacita Dean teilt er die Sparsamkeit der Mittel und die kinematographische Fähigkeit, Zeit zu verdichten. Latente Erotik und eine gewisse Bedrohlichkeit verbinden sein Werk mit dem von Douglas Gordon.

McQueens Filme kommen ohne Erzählstrang aus, sind reduziert auf ein Minimum an Handlung, hauptsächlich in Schwarzweiß gedreht und fast immer ohne Ton. Trotz der Schlichtheit der Handlung, auf der sie basieren – wie etwa Ringen (BEAR, 1993), Spazierengehen (JUST ABOVE MY HEAD, 1996), Beobachten (STAGE, 1996), Werfen (CATCH, 1997), Stillstehen (DEADPAN, 1997), Berühren (COLD BREATH, 2000) –, sind die Filme von einer subtilen Komplexität geprägt, die aus ungewöhnlichen Einstellungen, kreativer Schnitttechnik und faszinierender Spannung resultiert. Der zwischen Bewegung und Reglosigkeit alternierende Rhythmus, der für sein Werk so wesentlich ist, drückt sich vielleicht am anschaulichsten in DEADPAN aus, einer Hommage an Buster Keaton,

41/41 ZOO DIPTYCH

wo die Fassade eines Hauses immer wieder über dem Künstler zusammenstürzt, der dabei reglos und vollkommen aufrecht verharrt.

In der Montage verschiedener Themensequenzen stellt FIVE EASY PIECES (1995) einen formalen Gegensatz zum früheren und auch folgenden Schaffen von McQueen dar. Hier wirkt das, was er gefilmt hat, weniger wichtig als die Art, wie er es gefilmt hat. Sofort fallen die extremen Kameraeinstellungen auf, die von hoch über bis zu weit – manchmal direkt – unter einem Motiv wechseln, eine Technik, die sowohl an die Photographien Rodschenkos, wie an den deutschen expressionistischen Film erinnert. Man blickt zum Fuß einer Hochseilartistin hinauf, der vorsichtig auf dem Seil aufgesetzt wird, und spürt das Gewicht des unsichtbaren Körpers auf dem Seil und – im übertragenen Sinn – auf uns lasten. Dieses Bewusstsein unserer eigenen Körperlichkeit ist Teil der von McQueen beabsichtigten Wirkung: „Ich will die Leute in die Lage versetzen, dass sie beim Betrachten des Films sich selbst spüren."[9] Als nächstes schwingt unser Blickpunkt radikal in die Vogelperspektive, und wir sehen einer Gruppe von fünf Männern von oben beim Hula-Hoop-Tanz zu. Von hier aus verdichtet sich das Bild

zu einer graphischen Abstraktion rotierender Kreise, die eher Duchamps ROTORELIEFS als einer unschuldigen Spielszene ähneln. Schnitt zum nächsten Teil, wo Winkel und Stimmung wieder anders sind: Diesmal ragt ein Mann, der Künstler selbst, bedrohlich vor uns auf, sein Spiegelbild in einer Pfütze reflektiert. In einem Akt von schockierender und tabuverletzender Verachtung uriniert er in die Pfütze und damit scheinbar auf uns, während er gleichzeitig das Abbild mutwillig zerstört und in Wellen auflöst. Wie in COLD BREATH, einem Film, der den Künstler in Nahaufnahme beim zärtlichen Streicheln seiner Brustwarze zeigt, soll uns die körperliche Nähe zu etwas so zutiefst Intimem peinlich berühren. Durch die dezidiert monumentale und skulpturhafte Art, in der McQueen Einstellung und Positionierung von Bildern vornimmt und die Dimension mit extremen Kamerawinkeln überhöht, wird das klaustrophobische Gefühl, das der Künstler so geschickt inszeniert, noch zusätzlich gesteigert.

McQueens Filmen gelingt es, das Poetische mit dem streng Formalistischen, das Erotische mit dem Selbstbezüglichen zu verknüpfen. Selten länger als zehn Minuten und meist im Loop abgespielt, evozieren sie ein

Victor Burgin

Gefühl von Wiederholung und Kreisbewegung. McQueen modelliert Zeit wie eine unendlich formbare Substanz, die Handlung verspricht, dieses Versprechen aber nie einlöst.

Wie wir gesehen haben, beziehen sich die in Double Vision gezeigten Arbeiten manchmal direkt (Tacita Dean, Stephen Willats, Willie Doherty) oder indirekt (Victor Burgin, Mat Collishaw) auf deutsche Orte und Begebenheiten, erweitern diesen Ausgangspunkt aber immer zu eine universalen Erfahrung. Überdies handelt es sich bei einem Großteil der Ausstellung um neuere Arbeiten, die diese Verbindungen auf weniger augenfällige Weise deutlich machen, weil sie zwar von Ideen und Inspirationen zeugen, die erstmals während des Auslandsaufenthalts entwickelt oder gefestigt wurden, deren Ausführung jedoch zuweilen später stattfand.

Durch die enorme Freiheit, finanzielle Sicherheit sowie technische Hilfestellung seitens des DAAD hatten die Künstler oft das Gefühl, unbefangener experimentieren zu können, in ihrer Arbeit neues Terrain zu beschreiten und gleichzeitig mit ihrer Gemeinschaft auf Zeit neue Verbindungen einzugehen, die in manchen Fällen bis heute bestehen. So ist – obgleich es sich bei Double Vision doch noch um eine „nationale" Ausstellung handelt – ein Großteil der Arbeiten tief durchdrungen von den heterogenen Prozessen, die die Existenz als Ausländer im fremden Land mit sich bringt.

42-45 NIETZSCHE'S PARIS, 1999
single screen video projection
DVD 8 minute programme loop,
colour, NTSC stereo
Courtesy of the artist

Anmerkungen

1 Richard Hamilton, In: Hans Jörg Meyer, Hg., *Richard Hamilton, New Technology and Printmaking*, London, 1998, S. 35. Vgl. dazu: Dieter Schwarz, „Richard Hamilton: Interiors", in: *Richard Hamilton: Subject to an Impression*, Kunsthalle Bremen, 1998.

2 „In Stereoscopic Vision: A Dialogue between Jane and Louise Wilson and Lisa G. Corrin", Serpentine Gallery Ausstellungsbroschüre, London, 1999.

3 Victor Burgin, in: *British Artists in Berlin*, Ausstellungskatalog, Goethe-Institut London, 1981, o. S.

4 Victor Burgin, in: *Shadowed*, Architectural Association, London, 2000, S. 150.

5 Einigen dieser Überlegungen liegt ein Vortrag zugrunde, den Victor Burgin am 10. Oktober 2000 vor der Londoner Architectural Association über sein Werk gehalten hat.

6 Tacita Dean, „The English Patient", in: *The Independent*, 3. Februar 2001.

7 Seine Nachforschungen führten Willats in den frühen achtziger Jahren in die britische Punkszene und in verschiedene Szenen der Londoner Subkultur.

8 Stephen Willats, *Leben in vorgegebenen Grenzen – 4 Inseln in Berlin*, Ausstellungskatalog, Nationalgalerie Berlin, 1980-81, zit. nach dem englischen Originalmanuskript, das mir der Künstler zur Verfügung stellte.

9 Steve McQueen, zit. v. Richard Cork, „That's the way, Steve, you get it off your chest", in: *The Times*, 17. Mai 2000.

Richard Wentworth, BERLIN – 117 LANDMARKS / MARKSTEINE

This year the DAAD Berlin Artists' Programme looks back on its 35 year history, during which it has hosted guests from the fields of music, literature, film and the visual arts. It is an opportune moment to examine and assess the achievements of the programme. Looking back over the last years it is undoubtedly the case that the contribution of British artists in particular has been considerable. Artists who are now acclaimed internationally, all came to Berlin before they were the focus of such attention. The impressive list of artists from which Andrea Schlieker has made her selection for the exhibition, DOUBLE VISION, reads like a 'Who's Who' of contemporary British art.

DOUBLE VISION demonstrates how the concept of exchange, combined with a readiness to experience and investigate new surroundings, contains the potential to stimulate cultural and political dialogue in both art and society. It was Rachel Whiteread's stay in Berlin which gave impetus to her recently completed Holocaust memorial in Vienna's Judenplatz. But also in other, less spectacular works, the evolution of a new perspective and an awareness of another perception is discernible. This is reflected in the title DOUBLE VISION and expanded within the exhibition.

Like the DAAD programme itself, the exhibition is a result of a collaboration, though in this case between three institutions: the DAAD, the British Council and the Galerie für Zeitgenössische Kunst. All three institutions have been fully involved in the development of the project. We should like to thank first and foremost the artists, without whose vision this DOUBLE VISION could not of course have taken place. We should like to thank Andrea Schlieker, the curator of the exhibition, who has displayed extraordinary commitment to the project throughout, a continuation of her engagement with the DAAD programme as a jury member over seven years. We are also indebted to the Henry Moore Foundation for their generous contribution to the catalogue. Although the residencies of British artists on the DAAD programme originally took place in Berlin, and later Hanover and Munich we are delighted that the dialogue is now being extended to include another great German city.

Ulrich Podewils, DAAD, Berlin
Andrea Rose, British Council, London
Barbara Steiner, Galerie für Zeitgenössische Kunst, Leipzig

Andrea Schlieker

Parallel Encounters at Different Places*

* The title of this essay is borrowed from the title of a work by Stephen Willats, made for the GAK in Bremen, 1998.

Since the late 1980s the young British art scene has been the focus of international interest and acclaim. Celebrated worldwide and constantly reinventing itself, it shows no sign of running out of steam. No other country has enjoyed such enduring attention, for more than a decade, on the international contemporary exhibition circuit. Testimony is the stream of shows throughout the 1990s such as WITH ATTITUDE (Brussels 1992); BRILLIANT! (Minneapolis, 1995); MINKY MANKY (London 1995); LIFE/LIVE (Paris and Lisbon, 1995); FULL HOUSE (Wolfsburg, 1996); PICTURA BRITANNICA (Sydney, 1997); SENSATION (London, Berlin and New York, 1997-2000), to name just a few.

Yet national shows are often distrusted, even avoided by artists, who prefer instead to see their work within the larger international context. In recent years British artists have increasingly declined to exhibit under the much marketed "yBa" (young British artist) label, feeling that this narrow parameter suggests their work may be conformed to a neat slogan, framing it for easy consumption within a much hyped "sensational" packaging which belies their complex and multifarious identities, histories and objectives.

DOUBLE VISION goes beyond the familiar yBa formula: the fifteen artists shown here present a wider, cross-generational section of Britain's artistic landscape. But they have one thing in common: all spent time living and working in Germany, mainly in Berlin, as guests of the prestigious DAAD Artists' Programme. Their stay, whether for a few months or a whole year, always created a fruitful dialogue between artist and adopted city, generating fresh inspirational energies, providing a new and an invaluable "binary" vision, and often leaving an indelible mark on their work.

Britain has always been characterised by its carefully fostered insular attitude. Determined, for reasons of history as well as geography, to remain separate from "the continent", Britain has been content to be and appear to be forever locked in a "splendid isolation" (people in Britain still refer distantly to the rest of Europe as "the continent"). Only in the last fifteen years or so has a gradually increasing openness been discernible and a still rather hesitant sense of identity with European neighbours seem to be felt. From this climate of cultural introspection, the DAAD residency programme was a vital bridge that brought British artists to live and work

in a different country, often for the first time in their lives, and to immerse themselves in a foreign culture, language and politics. For many it was a revelation, not only opening up different ways of living but also offering them a critical, objectifying distance from their accepted sense of national identity. For each, the period of living and working in Germany became an important marker in his or her career, sometimes even a turning point. National stereotypes dissolve into another context, and chauvinistic navel-gazing gives away to a broader outlook.

Covering painting, sculpture, photography, and installation as well as sound, film and video work, DOUBLE VISION showcases the work of some of the most consistently central figures of the contemporary British art scene. The selection of fifteen (out of more than forty) British artists who have enjoyed the privileges of the residency programme since the mid 1960s, offers at the same time a representative cross-section of recent British art history, drawing from wide ranges of generation, status and media.

Whilst some of the works shown are made in direct response to the experience of living abroad, it seemed too restrictive and pedantic to make this an exclusive criterion. Some of these have had plenty of exposure before, and it was clearly more important to represent current practice (especially of artists whose residencies were completed 20 or 30 years ago) by showing new or recent work, much of which still betrays vestiges of concepts and techniques first developed during the DAAD year.

The diversity of artistic positions, as well as their common root in the DAAD scholarship programme, prevents a strictly thematic exhibition, but in the freedom of a non-chronological reading a number of connecting motifs can be found criss-crossing the various exhibits, creating not a single streamlined argument, but rather a web of relations and juxtapositions.

Damien Hirst is no doubt the most widely known of the so-called Brit-pack artists, identified with his flamboyant, *coup de théâtre* gestures of slicing whole cows or pigs and preserving them in formaldehyde. It was Hirst who launched the yBa phenomenon in 1988 with his now legendary exhibition FREEZE. With ingenious curatorial finesse and a real sense of showmanship Hirst thus provided the platform from which his fellow artists

BUBBLEHOUSE (EXTERIOR), 1999
R Type photograph
99 x 14. 5 cm

DISAPPEARENCE AT SEA II
(VOYAGE DE GUÉRISON), 1997
16 mm colour anamorphic film
Optical Sound 4 mins

launched their international careers, ironically leaving Hirst (– who at that stage showed some rather modest coloured constructivist boxes) behind.

It was only after he exhibited the spectacular A THOUSAND YEARS in 1990 (his first, rather operatic reflection on the eternal cycle of birth and death demonstrated by flies breeding inside a cow's head and their eventual extermination by insectocutor) that the focus shifted. Since then he has proved that he has the gift constantly to surprise. He has expanded into film, design and advertising, always tenaciously holding on to his central position. In spite of the kaleidoscopic nature of his work, certain formal elements have remained constant within the parameter of ever changing variations, such as his spot paintings and his cabinets, examples of both are on show in DOUBLE VISION. Whether he uses dead cows or live exotic butterflies, from his unorthodox organic material Hirst manages to elicit the visceral and aggressive as well as the romantic and lyrical. His is an enduring and ever-surprising exploration of his favoured themes of love and death.

The residency in Berlin in 1994 came at a pivotal point in Hirst's career, and consolidated his international reputation. "I love Berlin and Berlin loves me" (in slight adaptation of the Beuyssian title) would be a fitting epitome of his time there, which culminated with a dramatic butterfly-corridor installation at the DAAD galleries.

In DOUBLE VISION, Hirst's ongoing essay on vanity and the human condition takes the form of a large glass and steel wall-cabinet, STRIPTEASER (1996), containing two (plastic) human skeletons and an array of surgical instruments. Hirst first used surgical instruments in WHEN LOGICS DIE in 1991, a rather gruesome and graphic allusion to suicide. The skeletons, presumably those of a man and a woman, each isolated in its own glass coffin, and conjoined in death by two double containers full of the paraphernalia of modern medicine (like "gifts" in ancient burial rites), are a dispassionate yet melancholy statement of evanescence and futility.

Shelving systems with neatly displayed objects – be they beautiful (fish, glasses, shells) or repellent (cigarette butts, animal organs) – abound in Hirst's work and betray his fascination with taxonomies and systems of classification (not unlike his contemporaries Douglas Gordon and Simon Patterson). Together with his claus-

trophobic glass and steel cages, each of these wall-containers also acts as latter-day *memento mori*, reminding us of the transience of life and our feeble ways of shortening and prolonging it.

Dualisms like life and death, good and evil, love and hate also underpin much of the work of Douglas Gordon. For the Münster Skulpturen-Projekte in 1997, for example, he juxtaposed in a dark and dank pedestrian underpass two well-known cinematic stories, THE SONG OF BERNADETTE and THE EXORCIST. By projecting the two films simultaneously from both sides on to a single screen he metaphorically and literally fused heaven and hell.

Gordon is no stranger to Leipzig, having shown his film work there twice before, most memorably in 1995 when his now legendary film 24 HOUR PSYCHO was projected in the vast hall of Leipzig's central station. This slowed down and soundless version of Hitchcock's classic launched his international career.

By manipulating found film material (which can include medical archive footage or out takes from popular television serials) Gordon reveals unexpected layers of meaning. Psychological nuances, erotic ambiguities or moral dilemmas unfold from slowed down and muted appropriated film fragments.

Emphasis on personal and collective memory is another important aspect of Gordon's work. This he explores not only in the film and video works but, prior to this and still continuing, in his numerous text and action works. LIST OF NAMES (begun in 1990), the epic and ever-growing wall drawing recording the names of all people Gordon remembers to have met, fixes fugitive memory through text. Other works, such as SOMETHING BETWEEN MY MOUTH AND YOUR EAR (1994) and WORDS AND PICTURES (1996, shown in Leipzig during MOVING IMAGES, 1999), did the same using sound (music) and vision (films) respectively.

Like his contemporaries Damien Hirst and Mat Collishaw, Gordon places (simulated) violence and eroticism at the forefront of several works, yet deals with them in a perhaps more playful, ironic or "psychologising" way (see DIVIDED SELF, 1996). In his sound work WHAT YOU WANT ME TO SAY (1998) the artist can be heard murmuring "I love you" from a dozen loudspeakers placed randomly around the room. The psychologically revealing

FERNSEHTURM, 2001
16 mm-film, optical sound,
44 minutes
Courtesy of the artist,
Frith Street Gallery, London, and
Marian Goodman Gallery,
New York/Paris

title instantly undermines belief in the message and sabotages any sense of truth. And yet it seems impossible not to succumb to the hypnotic lure of the repeated profession. This ironic play on our desire to love and be loved (even beyond reason and to the point of self-deception) is also given characteristically acerbic form in Damien Hirst's I'LL LOVE YOU FOREVER (1994): a padlocked steel cage, containing a gas mask and medical waste in rows of brightly coloured buckets which display large "danger" signs.

The notion of "interiors", their significance and definition, is explored in very different ways by Richard Hamilton, Rachel Whiteread, Richard Wilson, Richard Wentworth and Jane and Louise Wilson. **Richard Hamilton**'s wide-ranging and intensely pursued interests (from science and technology to consumerism and advertising, from product design, typography and his preoccupation with the work of Duchamp to politics and power) have made the precursor of British Pop, whose work has remained consistently challenging and fresh, into one of the most formidable, versatile and influential figures in 20th century British art.

Hamilton spent several months of 1974 in Berlin, culminating in a large solo-show at the National Gallery. Whilst living in Berlin he continued his preoccupation with the domestic interior in a number of works based on photographs taken in René Block's apartment ("Berlin Interiors"). This is a theme that began with his pivotal collage of 1956 "Just what is it that makes today's homes so different, so appealing".

Hamilton's gift of continually re-inventing himself, even at the age now of 79, was particularly evident at the last Kassel Dokumenta in 1997. There he collaborated with Ecke Bonk on the highly sophisticated and technically complex THE TYPOSOPHIC PAVILION and also showed his astounding installation, SEVEN ROOMS (first seen at Anthony d'Offay Gallery, London 1995). This ambitious computer-aided photographic fusion of the interior of his London gallery with the interior of his Oxfordshire farmhouse, which emerges almost as some kind of a metaphorical self-portrait, is the starting point for all three of his very recent paintings in DOUBLE VISION.

But whilst the SEVEN ROOMS displayed contemplative, still-life like spaces devoid of human presence, Hamilton has here inserted the figure as central motif.

53

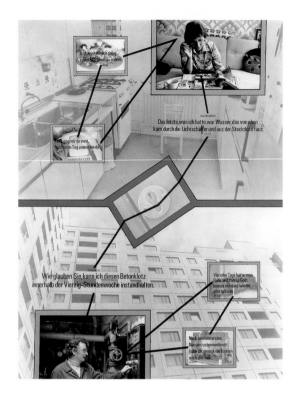

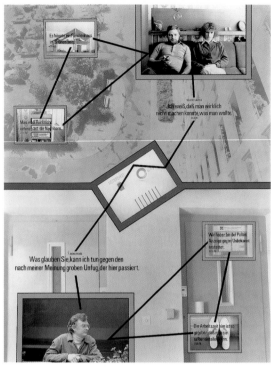

As Hamilton explains himself when he discusses the print version of THE PASSAGE OF THE BRIDE: "As part of a plan to populate the SEVEN ROOMS, a friend offered to model in the house from which they derive. Kodak again lent a camera and I made many photographs which could instantly be viewed on the computer monitor. (...) The passage source has a full-size pencil drawing of the lower part of Marcel Duchamp's LARGE GLASS, hanging on the west wall. Since the drawing was too faint to appear on the original photograph, I scanned a transparency of the Duchamp Apparatus into the Paintbox, applied perspective, and ghosted it in to replace the invisible drawing. (...) One of the digital photographs showed the model reading a letter by the window. The figure was too remote so I brought her closer and then placed a laterally reversed copy in the picture. (...) Seeing the reflection of the nude in the Duchamp context, the reflected figure appeared redundant."[1] With their Broodthaersian reference in the title, the bathroom paintings FIG 1 and FIG 2 are similarly based on a complex process and layering technique involving photography (this time the model is his wife, the artist Rita Donagh), computer manipulation, and final return of the image to paint and canvas.

The notion of interiority is fundamental to **Rachel Whiteread**'s work. From a starting point of ordinary domestic objects – a bed, a wardrobe, even a waterbottle – for her mimetic yet powerfully transforming casts, she not only explores the interiors of our domestic spaces in general but also the interior voids of the objects the spaces contain. Using translucent or opaque materials – such as plaster, rubber or resin – to define their negative space, the sculptures have both a familiar and a spectral appearance. This materialisation of space, of the void, the simultaneous absence and presence of a thing, articulates the core of Whiteread's endeavour. The memory of time past is hermetically sealed within each work, encapsulating notions of mortality and the *memento mori*. It is interesting that Hirst and Whiteread, connected by status, age and friendship, should both deal with a similar theme, yet use such opposite moods and means of expression. A sense of loss pervades the work of both, yet whilst Hirst evinces rage, horror and drama, Whiteread offers melancholy, silence and austerity.

Whiteread came to Berlin in 1992 and stayed for eighteen months. It was a particularly fruitful and inspirational time. For an artist who pursues the notion of

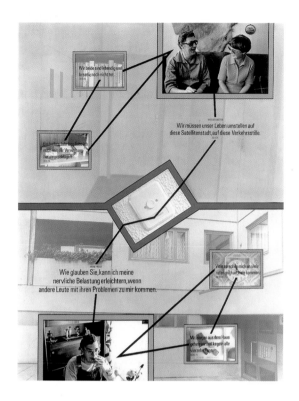

EINE POSTMODERNE LEBENSFORM,
1992/93
2 photo panel work
photographs, acrylic paint, letraset
text and mixed media
126 x 76.5 cm each
Courtesy the artist and
Galerie Thomas Schulte, Berlin

58/59 WIE ICH ENTDECKE, DASS
WIR VON ANDERN ABHÄNGIG SIND,
1979/80
3 photo panel work
photographs, letraset text, mixed
media on card, framed with perspex
130 x 98 cm each
Courtesy the artist and
Galerie Thomas Schulte, Berlin

memory with such poetic intensity, the city of Berlin provided a rich foil for and background to her own investigations. As she stated on several occasions, Whiteread would never have felt able to accept the prestigious but enormously daunting invitation from Vienna in 1996 to design a Holocaust memorial for one of its central squares (Judenplatz), had she not had the experience of living and working in a city redolent with the vestiges of recent history. Whilst investigating the architecture of war and death, Whiteread produced a prolific output of sculptures and drawings. One of the most important (and for the artist personally significant) pieces made during that time was UNTITLED (CONCAVE AND CONVEX BEDS) 1992, two corresponding mattress pieces that appear like contorted bodies writhing on the floor.

For DOUBLE VISION, Whiteread has made a ghostly echo of a room, with references to bookshelves, tables, floor and light switches. UNTITLED (STORIES) 1998, emerged, together with a number of other book and library sculptures, from the procrustinations surrounding the Vienna memorial. The three horizontal bars of delicately graded pastel stripes – traces of the more gaudy hues of the paperbacks from which they were

cast – remind us that she initially trained as a painter and make this one of her most lyrical pieces. Formally, the cuboid form of UNTITLED (SIX SPACES), 1994, recalls the language of minimalism as well as the ancient shape of a mausoleum. Its seductive luminosity is multiplied further in the grand UNTITLED (ONE HUNDRED SPACES), 1995. UNTITLED (CAST CORRIDOR) is one of Whiteread's most recent pieces, made in cast iron and then patinated. Here the references to minimalism, and especially the work of Carl André, are particularly strong. Yet whilst André's floor tiles have the seamless finish of mass production and speak of the generic, Whiteread's corridor, painstakingly hand-cast, is imbued with history and the particular. With its sensual and uneven surface (which people's footsteps will still change over time), Whiteread has shaped a place of memory, a discreet imprint of the presence of the past.

The use of domestic objects as trigger for collective memory and personal history is a trajectory that connects Whiteread's work with that of Richard Wentworth. Wentworth, who has been crucial and pioneering in his role as artist as well as teacher (at London's Goldsmith

ES IST SOWEIT NORMAL, ICH KENNE
DAS ANDERE LEBEN HALT NUR VON ERZÄHLUNGEN

MAN WÄCHST AUF, INTERESSEN ÄNDERN SICH,
ABER ALLE SIND GENAUSO GEBLIEBEN, WIE SIE WAREN

DIE SCHRANKWAND SIEHT AUCH FAST AUS WIE EIN TOWER DAS GEHT ALLES SO IN DIESE RICHTUNG

ICH WILL ES NICHT ALS IRGENDWELCHE MATTSCHEIBE SEHEN. ICH KANN JA DAS FENSTER AUFMACHEN, DANN KANN ICH ALLES SPÜREN

College, cradle for the generation of now acclaimed young British artists), first emerged in the late 1970s along with other British sculptors whose work focused on the everyday object. Wentworth's sculpture has always been marked by the use of the simple, even archetypal "thing". Culled primarily from the world of home and garden, his objects often refer to ancient forms. As with Whiteread, it is important for Wentworth that the object has been used, handled, and shows traces of use, thereby articulating our relationship with the object. While rarely interfering with the objects, he manages to achieve a radical change in our perception of their ordinariness, transmogrifying them into intriguing visual conundrums.

Wentworth's sculptures exude playfulness, magic and an irreverent sense of humour. For his exhibition TRAVELLING WITHOUT A MAP at Kunstwerke in 1994, at the end of his year-long residency, he created one of his visually most intriguing and at the same time surreally witty installations: a forest of differently shaped and coloured wooden poles seemingly held in vertical equilibrium by a variety of "props" beneath (books) and above (plates). As visitors had to wear hard hats whilst negotiating the multitude of poles, a sense of the precariousness and haphazardness of the installation increased. This feeling was reinforced as an association with the classic circus act of swirling plates on swivelling rods involuntarily sprang to mind (only here Wentworth used the plates upside down ...).

Plates are of course an old favourite in the Wentworthian repertoire of objects. Their fragility, varied form, special local design and vernacular colouring are just as important to Wentworth as their basic daily function. Like a conjurer, he would transform them into bilious clouds (CUMULUS, 1991), an undulating wave defying gravity (FLIGHT, 1999), or a landscape, as shown here with SPREAD (1997). The neo-baroque room seems a perfect foil for Wentworth's light-handed play with memory and history.

Wentworth is quintessentially an urban *flâneur*, a chronicler of our human codes of behaviour (especially in their different cultural guises), our odd ways of doing things and finding practical if ideosyncratic solutions. His photographic series MAKING DO & GETTING BY shows his keen eye for life's absurdities, coincidences and paradoxes, right around the globe. These images are

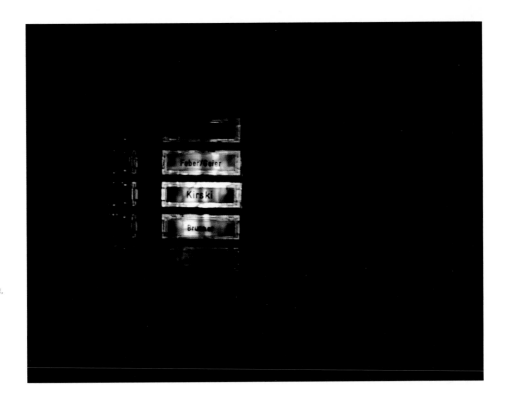

EXTRACTS FROM A FILE,
2000
black and white
photographs
mounted on
aluminium
45 x 60 cm each
Courtesy Galerie
Peter Kilchmann,
Zurich

immensely entertaining as well as strangely comforting
in their quixotic humanness. Wentworth extended this
series whilst living in Germany with 117 LANDMARKS,
another kaleidoscope of well-observed, all too familiar
tautologies and bizarre Germanisms, providing visual
anecdotes at once embarrassing, endearing and universal.

The motif of the interior is continued with **Jane and
Louise Wilson**'s large photo and video installations. These
explore specific places of power via the anatomy of their
architecture, combining form and function with the psychological "aura" of the buildings. A strange Hitchcockian
ambiance pervades all their work; it appears to produce a
sense of either apprehension or shocked aftermath of an
unspecified violent act. The Wilsons, who have been col-
laborating since 1989, share with Douglas Gordon this
interest in the psychological dimension and the nature of
perception whilst their fascination with the uncanny
links them with Mat Collishaw.

Their DAAD residency, in both Hanover and Berlin,
led to the making of their perhaps most famous film to
date: STASI CITY (1997), a turning point in their career.

Filmed in the former East German secret police head-
quarters and prison at Hohenschönhausen, it was the
first of a series of complex multi-screen video projections that focus on the interplay of individual and society, and the mechanisms of control. Having hitherto
chosen private, anonymous locations, such as abandoned flats or seedy hotel rooms, with STASI CITY they
shifted the mysterious and haunted quality of their interiors towards the public arena. "In Berlin we became particularly aware of historical architecture connected to
the Cold War. The political distinctions between East and
West Germany were focused on the meaning embedded
in buildings, what certain sites represented."[2] In their
most recent film, STAR CITY (2000) – which, together
with GAMMA (1999) and PARLIAMENT (1999) is the fourth
multi-screen video work investigating places of power –
we are taken inside a Russian space-training centre near
Moscow. The viewer is taken on another mesmerising
visual journey through what was during the Soviet era
essentially a hidden city, but has now become more
accessible, especially since the collaboration here
between American and Russian space agencies. Continuing differences between the two superpowers are

subtly referred to in the opening sequence of the film, where Russian and American on-site housing facilities are contrasted. The camera moves inside and we are gaining a glimpse inside depopulated, secret rooms and passages, culminating in the once state of the art hydro laboratory designed to simulate zero gravity – a site signalling not only rigorous training and research but also the national ambition and utopian dream to conquer space. Interiors echoing with ghostly emptiness and the sense of gloomy abandon are projected onto four screens, creating a stereoscopic effect and enveloping the viewer in this disorientating vision of dystopia.

Preoccupation with architectural spaces and their historical, political and social meaning is continued in this exhibition in the films of Victor Burgin and Tacita Dean, as well as in the photographic work of Stephen Willats and Willie Doherty, all of which is shown upstairs. **Victor Burgin** became known in the 1970s for his black and white photo-text pieces with their recurrent themes of voyeurism, surveillance, the city and alienation, combined with their referencing of classic cinematic traditions. Whilst in Berlin in 1978 he created the photo-

graphic series of eight diptychs entitled Zoo 78, a "dramatisation of certain concerns of sexual-political theory within an arena (Berlin) whose physical, political and historical structure is uniquely fitted to the staging of those concerns."[3]

In DOUBLE VISION, Victor Burgin is represented by NIETZSCHE'S PARIS (1999), a sumptuous single-screen video projection which takes its cue from a fateful historical encounter between Friedrich Nietzsche, Lou Andreas Salomé and Paul Rée in Leipzig in 1882. The plan was to create an intellectual *ménage à trois*, in communal living-quarters in Paris. Having met in Leipzig to finalise the arrangements, Nietzsche finds himself inexplicably abandoned by the other two, whom he mistakenly believes have fled to Paris. Yet this dramatic storyline is entirely withheld in the film, together with any depiction of Leipzig. Instead, we encounter computer-manipulated, depopulated images of the Parisian Bibliothèque Nationale. Burgin writes: "Though it ended in bitter estrangement, the short-lived relationship between Nietzsche and Salomé had passed through an idyllic space of intimacy during the three weeks in August they spent together debating philosophy in the forest of

Kreisbohrung beobachtet auf einer
Berliner Baustelle in der Nähe der
Potsdamer Straße, 1992
Core-drilling observed on a Berlin
building site near Potsdamer Straße,
1992

Richard Wilson

Tautenberg. The historical association between forests, gardens and learning is exploited by Dominique Pérrault in the recently completed Bibliothèque Nationale de France. Pérrault's sunken forest garden at the centre of the site has been appropriately described by one commentator as 'an untouchable Eden from which researchers and members of the public are barred.' In memory of Nietzsche's edenic period with the unattainable Lou it is the Paris site that appears in the work."[4]

In the film, sections of the austere architecture are spliced with short glimpses of a woman in nineteenth century dress, sitting very still on a bench in a lush green park or forest. This collision of different moments of time is emphasised by the use of black and white for one sequence, and colour for the other. The overlay of baroque music fragments (from Handel's ALCINA towards the beginning and his ARIODANTE towards the end of the loop) is particularly apt, as the architectural quality of the music synchronises with shots of the building and, furthermore, as both opera fragments thematise love triangles. But Burgin pushes the dichotomies even further: the tranquillity of images and music is juxtaposed with the emotional turbulence of the referenced characters; the rationalism of the modernist architecture is eclipsed by the irrationalism of the caged trees which seem to work as a metaphor for failed utopian concepts.[5]

NIETZSCHE'S PARIS is part of a series of recent video works, which are all connected by the use of opera fragments, spoken text in the original language and historical connotations via text, music and costume (LOVE LETTERS, 1997; LICHTUNG, 1998-99; ANOTHER CASE HISTORY, 1999; WATERGATE, 2000; ELECTIVE AFFINITIES, 2001).

The notion of a failed utopia expressed through an architectural icon is also taken up in **Tacita Dean**'s latest film FERNSEHTURM. Shot on a perfect summer evening last year from within the revolving restaurant, set sky-high above the streets of Berlin, it charts forty-four minutes of its hustle and bustle, from sunset to nightfall. The television tower in Alexanderplatz, situated in the heart of the former East German capital and one of the city's most famous landmarks, is arguably the most potent symbol of the former GDR's national identity, an enduring reminder of its hopes and aspirations. At the same time, the tower hints at continuing differences

SLICE OF REALITY,
Millennium Dome London, 2000

between the two parts of the city: it is a favourite tourist attraction for East Germans, but is largely ignored by those from the West. Moreover, it may be seen as perhaps another sign of change and East/West contrast that, since unification, the rotation speed of the restaurant has been doubled. It took a contemplative sixty minutes for a complete round; now it is thirty.

Initially uneasy about the propriety for a foreigner, who had come to Germany so recently, to make a film about a building loaded with cultural and political significance, Dean soon felt utterly seduced by the aptness of the tower for her work. FERNSEHTURM is a conceptually logical extension for her. She has made a number of films that focus on architectural anachronisms or metaphors of dashed hopes and lost causes, such as BUBBLEHOUSE (1999), or SOUND MIRRORS (1999); in DISAPPEARANCE AT SEA (1996), perhaps her most haunting work, she not only focuses on another nostalgic architectural structure, a lighthouse, but also selects the same poignantly emotive moment when day passes into night.

The artist wrote about the television tower in a recent newspaper article: "Built at a time when we believed in space travel, it was futuristic and bold, and yet its decor and optimism is locked in the Sixties. The revolving sphere in space is still our best image of the future and yet it has become a period concept." [6]

Most mesmerising in this work is the changing atmosphere, the sense of light, sound and space inside the restaurant. The constant element in this web of shifting coordinates is the majestic band of slanting window-frames, itself echoing the sequential rhythm of a film-strip, and the assured efficiency of the black and white clad, old-style waiters. We are taken through a complete cycle of the restaurant's evening routine, from empty to full to empty again, noisy to silent, light to dark, from infinite daylight views to the dark inwardness of its night-time space. In spite of the ordinariness, even banality, of the café operation, the scenario has a hypnotic effect which translates into something universal. When the rays of the setting sun transform a glass of wine into a glowing vessel of shimmering iridescence, when the scene constantly moves in and out of shade, Dean captures moments of the sublime in the commonplace delights of eating and drinking. The film appears as a celebration of the transformative qualities of light, of the passing of time made palpable with every new

68/69 Bottom Drawer 1, 2000
metal filing cabinet
133 x 75 x 55 cm
Courtesy Richard Wilson

Bottom Drawer 2, 2001
metal filing cabinet
133 x 62 x 47 cm
Courtesy Richard Wilson

Jamming Gears, 1996
Serpentine Gallery, London

rotation of the restaurant within its sphere and limitless space outside. Together with the dramatic shifts of light, Fernsehturm becomes a microcosm parallel to planetary movement.

Architecture as constituent of identity is also the basis for Stephen Willats' seminal practice. Delving directly into the social fabric of a city he works like an urban anthropologist, and his art is closely related to sociological studies. The results of his research, evolved from countless photographs and interviews, are presented in panels of diagrammatic photo-collages.

Willats anchors his wide-ranging projects in specific social groups. Most of his "fieldwork" has been conducted in areas of modernist social housing – another utopian dream of the 1960s and 70s – such as tower blocks, both in London and in tenement houses in Berlin, Eindhoven or New York.[7]

In Berlin in 1979-80 (and again on his return in 1992) Willats directed his research towards the main centres of social housing there, whilst focusing on themes of isolation and dependency: Märkisches Viertel and Gropiusstadt. In addition he chose an allotment and a

boutique to illustrate issues of escape and passivity respectively. After initial, often complicated attempts to make contact with people living or working in the various locations, and gaining their confidence to collaborate with him, Willats started the interview process: "The next stage involved making a tape recording with each participant (...) In the initial tape recording I asked very simple, descriptive questions about the environment and the activities that went on there (...) I then went on to photograph, in another session, the environment, objects within it and the participant (...) After I had sifted through my first set of documentations I then formulated for each participant ten questions which were directed specifically at the various concerns of each work (...) My documentations went on over an average six months period requiring five or six visits and, as a result, I got to know each participant and they got used to me, and were much more forthcoming and helpful in directing the documentation by telling me what I should photograph, and what they thought in their lives was important to my "work"(...). While the decisions of what references were to be used in the [final] work were mine, with the advice of the assistant helping me, the

NEON RICE FIELD, 1993
Rice, clear red neons
1500 x 450 cm
Courtesy Stephen Friedman Gallery,
London

71 ATOPIA, 1997
DAAD, Berlin, Jägerstraße
pigeon sticks, 2800 x 2800 cm

72/73 ATOPIA, 2001
steel shelving, polybutadeine
synthetic rubber, daadgalerie,
Kurfürstenstraße
300 x 300 x 200 cm
Courtesy Vong Phaophanit and
Stephen Friedman Gallery, London

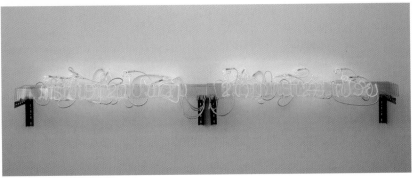

UNTITLED, 1996
Laotian words in clear blue neon,
glass, painted steel
242 x 26 x 140 cm
Courtesy Stephen Friedman Gallery,
London

final decision was that of the participant. (...) The range of response varies considerably, the man in the tower thought my proposals about his life were too negative and changed quite a lot of the quotations to be more positive, while the Housemaster [at the Märkisches Viertel] accepted everything as it was, saying: 'That's real life, that's how it is.'"[8]

Willats' interactive, participatory working model, which he started in the mid 1960s, has made him a pioneer of a democratic form of art that understands the origination of a work as dependent on interaction between people. The artist as catalyst, rather than as producer of autonomous objects, privileging the ordinary and peripheral, is a concept of distinctive currency in the art of the last decade.

An emphasis on seemingly dispassionate documentary reportage methods can also be observed in the videos and photographs of Willie Doherty. Like the work of Willats, Doherty's images allude to the specific and general, individual and universal. Yet what singles out Doherty first and foremost is his Irish nationality and therefore the political perspective that underpins his

work. Most of his photographs and video projections are taken in and around his native Derry, or Londonderry, the colonial name by which this old walled city is better known. Doherty alludes to, yet never takes sides in, the continuing intransigences of the Irish conflict, and this non-criticising and non-idealising stance led Carolyn Christov Bakargiev to call his work "meta-political". Derry has of course for decades been one of the main targets for sectarian violence: it was here that the notorious Bloody Sunday killings occurred in 1972.

Doherty's images show a preference for the non-place, the anonymous no-man's land marked by abandonment and dereliction, between the rural and urban. Spending his entire life in a city as polarised and volatile as Derry has sharpened his awareness for the psychological effect of borders and for the clichéd construction of the "enemy" or "terrorist" identity. In an early slide-text installation from 1990, for example, SAME DIFFERENCE, he showed how perception can be manipulated by language and insinuation. It seemed particularly poignant, therefore, to invite Willie Doherty to come and live in another city, for so many years marked by its walled status and its inherent sense of duality, and to continue in

Berlin his investigations into the contextualisation and framing of national identities.

Since the mid 1990s Doherty's video pieces and colour cibachromes have been mapping an increasingly indistinct terrain. They still deal with subliminal fears and anxieties, but present a more pronounced ambiguity of place and position. His latest work on show here, EXTRACTS FROM A FILE, is a series of 40 small photographs of windswept staircases and occasionally lit windows taken at night in the streets of Berlin. After the complex multi-screen video installations of recent years EXTRACTS FROM A FILE signals a rigorous formal simplification as well as a return to Doherty's first photographic images in black and white – though these were overlaid with politically charged text and framed behind glass. This distancing device is removed here, and the unpopulated night scenes are so imbued with impenetrable, velvety blackness that any incident appears spectral. On closer inspection these are not the innocuous visions of an urban nocturnal *flâneur*. A more mysterious emotional climate unfolds. The impression is of covert surveillance; the psychological effect is of suspense; fear lurks in dark passageways. But then Doherty, like Tacita Dean, has

always been interested in blurring the distinction between fact and fiction, reportage and artifice, documentation and enigma.

References to architecture and domestic interiors resurface in the work of **Richard Wilson**, whose spliced, cut and dissected new furniture sculptures for DOUBLE VISION reveal, by constant reversal of inside and outside, what is normally hidden. Like Rachel Whiteread and Richard Wentworth, Wilson too, turns to the domestic or "homely" for inspiration. In his interventions chairs and filing cabinets, but also the domestic swimming pool, the garden shed or greenhouse, are suspended, filleted or inverted, presenting us with an experience or apprehension of risk, danger or the aftermath of violence.

For the recent Millennium Dome sculpture project Wilson produced perhaps one of his most spectacular pieces to date. He took, as tribute to the once vibrant history of merchant shipping on the Thames, the central "slice", including the bridge, through the hull of a huge 30 year old dredger and rested it in the Thames close to the river wall, the tide flowing through and in and out of the exposed skeleton. Situated on a cusp of land and

INFECTIOUS
FLOWERS II,
1996/97
wooden lightbox
with
photographic
transparency
50 x 50 x 10 cm

FLESHEATERS 1,
1999
Iris print,
101 x 76 cm

water, of object and architecture and past and present, SLICE OF REALITY was both melancholy and celebratory. Like his spiritual antecedent Gordon Matta-Clark, Wilson cuts, slices and drills into the architectural body, only to rearrange its segments in a disconcerting way. The experience of perceptual displacement was almost hallucinatory in his now legendary piece 20:50 where gallons of sump-oil provided a vast expanse of shining blackness that perfectly mirrored the ceiling, literally turning upside-down any attempt at a spatial reading. To disorientate his viewer by disrupting habitual patterns of perception is the aim that links all of Wilson's audacious installations.

Wilson is at his best when he is allowed to interfere directly with the architectural structure of a building. When the Serpentine Gallery invited him for their final exhibition before a major refurbishment programme, a *carte blanche* to do as he pleased with the building presented the ideal scenario. JAMMING GEARS, his exhibition there in 1996, was built almost entirely around an expectation of impending collapse. An invasion of fork-lift trucks and builders' cabins, tilted at dangerous angles as if a hurricane had blown through the gallery,

foreshadowed the planned renovation. In a gesture of apparent brutality and disrespect Wilson pierced a multitude of deep circular holes through the gallery's stone floor, through walls complete with bookshelves, even boring the ceiling through to the sky, thus making the building vulnerable but also opening views and vistas that established unexpected connections. Witnessing the intricacies of core-drilling on a typical Berlin building site during his DAAD scholarship was Wilson's inspiration for this outstanding work.

Emphasis on materiality, together with the delight in its transformative power and metaphorical meaning, can also be found in **Vong Phaophanit**'s work. Born in Laos, trained in France, but resident in Britain since 1986, Phaophanit began making installations from materials evoking his homeland, such as rice, bamboo, silk and rubber. At the same time, these organic substances, loaded with multiple cultural, historical and economic associations, were juxtaposed with (predominantly red) strips of fluorescent neon. Sometimes presented just in a straight line, as in NEON RICE FIELD, but more often forming words in Laotian script, the neon complements

BURNT ALMONDS
3D lenticular print
137 x 122 cm
Courtesy Modern Art, London

76/77 SHANGRI LA, 2001
video installation
acrylic, steel, cloth
240 x 130 x 130 cm
Courtesy Modern Art, London

the seductive materiality of the organic substances with an artificial glow and the notion of language – a language of course, which obstructs meaning for most viewers. Communication is deliberately withheld in the glowing haze of the text works.

Unreadability is occasionally intensified even further, when hundreds of blue neon words are haphazardly piled on top of each other in a long trench constructed beneath the gallery floor (AZURE BLUE BODY, 1994) or when Laotian script is stacked five layers deep in a recent untitled wall-piece. Light is a central feature in many of Phaophanit's works, engulfing viewers and transforming them into dazzlingly chromatic participants (not unlike Douglas Gordon's SOMETHING BETWEEN MY MOUTH AND YOUR EAR, where the spectator is plunged into a pool of blue light, the colour of memory.)

Since Phaophanit's stay in Berlin there has been a marked change and caesura in his work. His move from organic to synthetic material had a spectacular manifestation in his two venue show in Berlin in 1997, ATOPIA. In a rooftop installation thousands of white pigeon-sticks – the ubiquitous and rather brutal bird-deterrent on many public buildings – pierced the sky, transforming an ordinary blank expanse of flat roof into a magical and apparently dangerous white carpet, inviting yet barring access at the same time. It was while he was in Germany that Phaophanit first experimented with synthetic rubber. In the DAAD galleries he installed long rows of metal shelving, laden with three tons of polybutadeine, a slowly and salaciously oozing material, evoking some grotesquely mutating or decomposing creature. The associations with living, albeit alien, organisms, with a breed of a threatening, still unknown species, is uncanny and powerful. Phaophanit extends this idea for DOUBLE VISION, here constructing a massive tower laden with the eerie, dripping lumps of rubber which the visitor must carefully circumnavigate within the installation's narrow space. The sense of claustrophobia and the device of obstructing the viewer's path with some form of barrier are repeatedly found in his work (ASH AND SILK WALL; IN THE SHADOW OF WORDS; LITTERAE LUCENTES; WHAT FALLS TO THE GROUND BUT CAN'T BE EATEN?). In most cases, however, Phaophanit's barriers allow, even require passage and transition.

The eerie and bizarre is a quality markedly attractive to **Mat Collishaw**. His series of INFECTIOUS FLOWERS shows a

79-83 Five Easy Pieces, 1995
video installation, 16 mm b/w and
colour film/video transfer
7.34 minutes duration
Courtesy Marian Goodman Gallery,
New York and Paris,
Thomas Dane Ltd., London

Steve McQueen

Deadpan, 1997
16 mm black and white film,
video transfer (video still)

similar duality of beauty and disease, attraction and repulsion as Phaophanit's metamorphosing rubber sculptures. Collishaw's images, displayed in lightboxes, show close-ups of gorgeous flowers in full bloom. But a second glance reveals the menace they contain: digitally fused with images of various skin-disease conditions, the flowers degenerate into something abject and poisonous. This corruption of perfection and innocence is a common strategy in Collishaw's photographic work; pictures of exotic flowers, young sleeping girls or naked boys are instilled with a sense of malaise – the girls' sleep is revealed to be narcotic induced, the boys are surrounded by urban decay and destruction.

Thematically, Collishaw's work addresses notions of sexuality, violence and voyeurism as well as today's problems and questions of our own morality. His enormously varied output combines high and low tech, photography, video, projection and installation. Unusually for an artist of his generation his historical sources often stem from the 19th century. This is reflected in the many Victorian props he uses in his video installations, as well as in his choice of subject matter (Baron von Gloeden's images were the inspiration for his Ideal Boys series;

Wright of Derby's An Experiment on a Bird in the Air Pump for his video sculpture Antique).

His year in Berlin inspired him to develop his historically most specific work, Burnt Almonds, a series of 3-D lenticular prints, which, following an orgy of sex, alcohol and drugs in sinister bunkers, dramatically stage Nazi suicides at the moment of defeat in 1945. Rather than sober illustration of historical fact he gives us an operatic and squalid portrait of the end of the Third Reich.

For Double Vision Collishaw has made a new work, based on video footage shot at the Berlin Zoo during his residency. Shangri La is the vision of an earthly paradise and world peace where people of all ethnic backgrounds, in their national dress, are united for an idyllic *déjeuner sur l'herbe*. It could be seen as an idealistic and utopian counterpart to his works addressing the plight of people on the social periphery – the homeless and prostitutes. However, far from being a simple chronicler of modern life Collishaw sets his videos in the realm of the magical: the homeless person finds himself projected into a snow dome, the prostitute into the centre of an artificial lily on a pond, and Shangri La's illusionistic utopian picnic can only be discovered inside an old-fashioned, ram-

shackle tent. This dualism, juxtaposing innocence and experience, pastoral and urban, romantic and decadent, good and evil, real and imagined, feeds into all of Collishaw's work.

Although he is only 32, **Steve McQueen**'s films show a formidably assured handling of the medium. Strongly influenced by cinematic history, and foreign films in particular, McQueen has developed a compelling visual language and a highly sophisticated and individual style. Like Jane and Louise Wilson, he performs as actor in his films, but without in any way making the films "about" him. With Tacita Dean he shares an economy of means and the cinematographic ability to condense time. A latent eroticism and a sense of threat connect his work with that of Douglas Gordon.

McQueen's films are stripped of narrative, pared down to a minimum of incident, shot mainly in black and white, and almost always without sound. In spite of the simplicity of the actions on which they are based, like wrestling (BEAR, 1993), walking (JUST ABOVE MY HEAD, 1996), looking (STAGE, 1996), throwing (CATCH, 1997), standing still (DEADPAN, 1997), touching (COLD

BREATH, 2000), the films are characterised by a subtle complexity achieved by unusual framing, inventive editing and compelling suspense. The rhythm of alternating movement and stillness, so central to his work, is perhaps most quintessentially expressed in his tribute to Buster Keaton, DEADPAN, where the façade of a house repeatedly collapses over the artist, who remains motionless and perfectly upright.

In its montage of different thematic sequences FIVE EASY PIECES (1995) represents a formal contrast to McQueen's earlier and subsequent output. Here what he has filmed seems less important than how he has filmed it. What is immediately striking are the film's extreme camera angles, altering from high above to down below to underneath an image, a technique reminiscent both of Rodchenko's photographs as of German Expressionistic film. To look up at a tightrope walker's foot being carefully placed on a rope is to feel the weight of the invisible body bearing down on it and, by extension, on us. This awareness of our own physicality is part of McQueen's desired effect: "I want to put people in a situation where they're sensitive to themselves watching the piece."[9] Next, our point of vision is radically

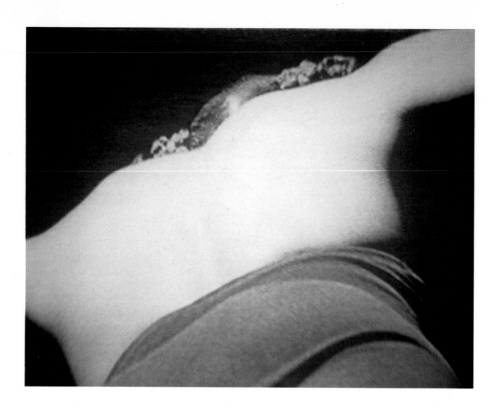

flipped to a bird's-eye perspective, and we look down on a group of five hula-hooping men. From here the image condenses to a graphic abstraction of rotating circles, closer to Duchamp's ROTORELIEFS than to a scene of innocent play. Cut to the next section, and angle and mood have changed again: now a man, the artist himself, is towering menacingly above us, his image reflected in a puddle. In an act of outrageous and taboo-breaking defiance he urinates into the puddle and thereby seemingly on us, whilst at the same time deliberately dissolving the image and shattering it into rippling waves. As in COLD BREATH, a film which shows the artist fondling his nipple in close-up, we are made to feel embarrassed by our physical proximity to something so profoundly intimate. Moreover, the decidedly monumental and sculptural quality of McQueen's framing and positioning of images, exaggerating scale with extreme camera angles, greatly heightens the sense of claustrophobia the artist so cunningly sets up.

McQueen's films manage to combine the poetic with the strictly formalist, the erotic with the self-referential. Rarely longer than ten minutes and mostly looped they create a sense of repetitiveness and circular-ity. McQueen moulds time like an infinitely pliable essence, appearing forebodingly to promise but never fulfilling action.

As we have seen, the works shown in DOUBLE VISION sometimes relate directly (Tacita Dean, Stephen Willats, Willie Doherty) or obliquely (Victor Burgin, Mat Collishaw) to German locations and events, yet they always transcend this starting point and move towards a universal experience. Moreover, a large part of the show consists of recent works that betray these links in a less obvious way, being testimony to ideas and inspirations first developed or consolidated, but not necessarily executed, whilst the artists were living abroad. Because of the immense freedom, financial security and technical support offered by the DAAD programme, artists often felt more at ease to experiment, to open up new territories in their work, and at the same time, whilst engaging with their adopted community, to forge new links which in many cases are sustained to the present day. Therefore, although DOUBLE VISION is still a "national" show, much of the work is deeply informed by the heterogeneous processes involved in being a foreigner abroad.

Footnotes

1 Richard Hamilton, in: *Richard Hamilton, New Technology and Print-making*, edition Hans Jörg Meyer (London) 1998, p. 35. See also Dieter Schwarz, "Richard Hamilton: Interiors", in: *Richard Hamilton: Subject to an Impression*, Kunsthalle Bremen 1998.

2 "In Stereoscopic Vision: A Dialogue between Jane and Louise Wilson and Lisa G.Corrin", Serpentine Gallery brochure, London 1999, unpaginated.

3 Victor Burgin, in: *British Artists in Berlin*, exhibition catalogue, Goethe Institute London, 1981, unpaginated.

4 Victor Burgin, in: *Shadowed*, Architectural Association, London 2000, p. 150.

5 Some of these thoughts are based on a lecture Victor Burgin gave about his work at the Architectural Association in London, 10 October 2000.

6 Tacita Dean, "The English Patient", *The Independent*, 3 February 2001.

7 In the early 1980s his investigations led Willats to the British Punk scene and various London club subcultures.

8 Stephen Willats, *Leben in vorgegebenen Grenzen – 4 Inseln in Berlin*, exhibition catalogue, Nationalgalerie Berlin, 1980-81; quoted from English original manuscript given to me by the artist.

9 Steve McQueen, quoted by Richard Cork, in "That's the way, Steve, you get if off your chest", *The Times*, 17 May 2000.

Victor Burgin

1941 Geboren / Born in Sheffield
1962-65 Royal College of Art, London
1965-67 Yale University, New Haven, Connecticut
1978 DAAD International Artists Programme, Berlin

Lebt und arbeitet / Lives and works in Paris and San Francisco

Ausgewählte Einzelausstellungen/ Selected Solo Exhibitions

2001 Fundació Antoni Tàpies, Barcelona
Nietzsche's Paris, Christine Burgin Gallery, New York
2000 *Nietzsche's Paris and Studies for Video*, Galerie Liliane & Michel Durand-Dessert, Paris
Nietzsche's Paris, Architectural Association, London
1999 *Lichtung, Weimar 99*, Weimar, Germany
The Glue Man and other studies for video, John Weber Gallery, New York
Love Stories #2 and Studies for Video, Museum Van Hedendaagse Kunste, Gent
1998-99 *Case History*, Yerba Buena Center for the Arts, San Francisco
Szerelmes Levelek/Love Letters, Mücsarnok Museum, Budapest
1998 *The Embrace and Studies for Video*, Galerie Fotohof, Salzburg
1996 *Love Stories*, John Weber Gallery, New York
1995 *The End*, University of Buffalo Art Gallery and the Research Center in Art + Culture
The End, John Weber Gallery, New York

Ausgewählte Gruppenausstellungen/ Selected Group shows

2000-01 *Media/Metaphor*, 46th Corcoran Biennial, Corcoran Gallery of Art, Washington DC
2000 *New Narrative Strategies*, Rencontres Internationales, Arles
1999 *Notorious*, Museum of Modern Art, Oxford. Tour to Sydney, Tokyo, Barcelona
1996-97 *Face à l'Histoire 1933-1966: L'artiste moderne face à l'événement historique*, Centre Georges Pompidou, Paris
1996 *Hall of Mirrors: Art and Film Since 1945*, the Museum of Contemporary Art/ the Temporary Contemporary, Los Angeles; Palazzo della Esposizione, Rome
1995-96 *3ʳᵈ Biennale de Lyon: installation, cinéma, vidéo, informatique*, Lyon (inaugural exhibition of the newly constructed Musée d'Art Contemporain de Lyon), France

Ausgewählte Bibliographie/ Selected Bibliography

2001 *Victor Burgin*, Fundació Antoni Tàpies, Barcelona, texts by Norman Bryson, Francette Pacteau, Peter Wollen and Victor Burgin
2000 *Shadowed*, Architectural Association, London, texts by Anthony Vidler and Victor Burgin
Victor Burgin: Robert Gwathmey Lectures, Cooper Union for the Advancement of Science and Art, New York

1997 *Venise*, Black Dog Publishing, London
1996 *In/ Different Spaces: place and memory in visual culture*, University of California Press, Berkeley and Los Angeles
Some Cities, University of California Press, Berkeley and Los Angeles and Reaktion Books, London
1995 *History Painting*, University at Buffalo Art Gallery/ Research Center in Art + Culture, Buffalo

Mat Collishaw

1966 Geboren / Born in Nottingham
1985-86 Trent Polytechnic, Nottingham
1986-89 Goldsmiths College, London
1998-99 DAAD International Artists Programme, Berlin

Lebt und arbeitet / Lives and works in London

Ausgewählte Einzelausstellungen/ Selected Solo Exhibitions

2001 Site Gallery, Sheffield
New Works, Modern Art, London
Ultra Violet Baby, 4 day film screening, Shoreditch Town Hall, London
Lux Gallery, London, part of the 'Pandeæmonium' Festival 2001
Bonakdar Jancou Gallery, New York
Galerie Raucci / Santamaria, Naples
2000 Museum of Contemporary Art, Warsaw
1999 Galeria Arte Moderna, Bologna
1998 Tanya Bonakdar Gallery, New York
Bloom Gallery, Amsterdam
1997 *Duty Free Spirits*, Lisson Gallery, London
Galerie Analix, Geneva
Ideal Boys, Gallerie Raucci/Santamaria, Naples, and Riding House Editions, London
1995 Camden Arts Centre, London

Ausgewählte Gruppenausstellungen/ Selected Group shows

2001 *Electronic Maple*, New York Centre for Media Arts, New York
Field Day: Sculpture from Britain, Taipei Fine Arts Museum, Taiwan
2000 *Greenhouse Effect*, Serpentine Gallery, London
1998-99 *Real/Life, New British Art*, Tochigi Prefectural Museum of Fine Arts; Fukuoka City Art Museum; Hiroshima City Museum of Contemporary Art; Museum of Contemporary Art, Tokyo; Aishiya City Museum of Art and History.
1998 *Pictura Britannica*, Museum of Contemporary Art, Sydney; Art Gallery of South Australia, Adelaide; City Gallery, Wellington, New Zealand
1996 *Sensation, Young British Artists from the Saatchi Collection*, Royal Academy of Art, London; Hamburger Bahnhof, Berlin; Brooklyn Museum of Art, New York
1996-97 *Live/Life*, Musée d'Art Moderne, Paris and Centro Cultural de Belem, Lisbon
1995 IV Istanbul Biennale, Istanbul
British Art Show 4, London, Manchester, Edinburgh and Cardiff

Brilliant! New Art from London, Walker Art Centre, Minneapolis; Museum of Fine Arts, Houston
Here and Now, Serpentine, London
Minky Manky, South London Art Gallery, London
1994 *Institute of Cultural Anxiety*, Institute of Contemporary Arts, London
1993 *Aperto*, XLV Venice Biennale, Venice
1988 *Freeze*, Surrey Docks, London

Ausgewählte Bibliographie/
Selected Bibliography

1997 *Mat Collishaw*, Artimo Foundation, Breda, Netherlands, text by John Thomson
1993 *Mat Collishaw*, Galerie Analix, Geneva, texts by Stuart Morgan, Françoise Jaunin, Mat Collishaw and an interview by Alison Sarah Jacques

Tacita Dean

1965 Geboren / Born in Canterbury
1985-88 Falmouth School of Art
1989-90 Greek Government scholarship to the Supreme School of Fine Art, Athens
1990-92 The Slade School of Fine Art
1994 Barclay's Young Artist Award, London
1997 Scriptwriter's Lab, Sundance Institute, Sundance, Utah
Nomination for the Turner Prize, Tate Gallery, London
1999 Artist in Residence, Wexner Center for the Arts, Columbus, Ohio
2000-01 DAAD International Artists Programme, Berlin

Lebt und arbeitet / Lives and works in Berlin

Ausgewählte Einzelausstellungen/
Selected Solo Exhibitions

2001 Marian Goodman, Paris
daadgalerie, Berlin
Museu d'Art Contemporani de Barcelona
Tate Britain, London
Melbourne International Biennial, Melbourne
FLOH, Frith Street Gallery, London
2000 Marian Goodman Gallery, New York
Museum für Gegenwartskunst, Basel
Friday/ Saturday, Millennium Sculpture Project, London
Sala Montcada de la Fundació "la Caixa", Barcelona
1998 Galerie Gebauer, Berlin
De Pont Foundation, Tilburg, Holland
Institute of Contemporary Art, Philadelphia
Madison Art Center, Wisconsin
Sadler's Wells, London
Marian Goodman Gallery, Paris
The Sea, with a Ship; afterwards an Island, Dundee Contemporary Arts, Scotland
1997 Witte de With Center for Contemporary Art, Rotterdam
The Drawing Room, The Drawing Center, New York
Frith Street Gallery, London
1996 *Foley Artist*, Art Now Room, Tate Gallery, London
1995 *Clear Sky, Upper Air*, Frith Street Gallery, London
Galerie 'La Box', Ecole National des Beaux Arts, Bourges, France

Ausgewählte Gruppenausstellungen/
Selected Group shows

2001 *Arcadia*, National Gallery of Canada, Ottowa
Yokohama International Triennale of Contemporary Art, Yokohama
2000-02 *Landscape*, British Council touring exhibition, ACC Gallery, Weimar, Germany and tour
New British Art 2000: Intelligence, Tate Britain, London
Vision and Reality, Louisiana Museum of Art, Louisiana, Denmark
1998 *Wounds: between democracy and redemption in contemporary art*, Moderna Museet, Stockholm
Turner Prize, Tate Gallery, London
1995 *British Art Show 4*, tour to London, Manchester, Edinburgh and Cardiff

Ausgewählte Bibliographie/
Selected Bibliography

2001 *Tacita Dean*, Sala Montcada de la Fundació "la Caixa", Barcelona
Tacita Dean, Tate Britain, London, texts by Stephen Deuchar, Clarrie Wallis, Sean Rainbird, Michael Newman, J.G. Ballard, Germaine Greer, Susan Stewart, Friedrich Meschede, Peter Nichols and Simon Crowhurst
Tacita Dean, Museu d'Art Contemporani de Barcelona, Barcelona
2000 *Tacita Dean*, Museum für Gegenwartskunst, Basel
1998 *Tacita Dean*, Institute of Contemporary Art, University of Pennsylvania, Philadelphia
1997 *Disappearance at Sea*, Edition Adelie, Limoges and L'Ecole Nationale de Bourges, France

Willie Doherty

1959 Geboren / Born in Derry, Northern Ireland
1977-78 Ulster Polytechnic, Jordanstown
1978-81 Ulster Polytechnic
1994 Nomination for the Turner Prize, Tate Gallery, London
1995 Awarded Glen Dimplex Artists Award, The Irish Museum of Modern Art, Dublin
1999-00 DAAD International Artists Programme, Berlin

Lebt und arbeitet / Lives and works in Derry

Ausgewählte Einzelausstellungen/
Selected Solo Exhibitions

2001 *Willie Doherty*, Matt's Gallery, London
Willie Doherty, Ormeau Baths Gallery, Belfast
Willie Doherty, The Brno House of Arts, Czech Republic
2000 *Blackspot*, Vancouver Art Gallery, Vancouver
Extracts from a File, daadgalerie, Berlin;
Kerlin Gallery, Dublin; Galerie Peter Kilchmann, Zurich;
Gesellschaft für Aktuelle Kunst, Bremen
1999 *Dark Stains*, Koldo Mitexelena Kulturunea, San Sebastian
Willie Doherty: new photographs and video, Alexander and Bonin, New York

True Nature, The Renaissance Society, Chicago
Somewhere Else, Tate Gallery, Liverpool; Museum of Modern Art, Oxford

1997 *same old story*, Matt's Gallery and tour
1996 *The Only Good One is a Dead One*, Fundaçao Calouste Gulbenkian, Lisbon; Galleria Emi Fontana, Milan
Willie Doherty, Musée d'Art Moderne de la Ville de Paris, Paris
In the Dark: Projected Works by Willie Doherty, Kunsthalle Bern; Kunstverein, Munich
1994 *At the End of the Day*, British School at Rome
Willie Doherty, Kerlin Gallery, Dublin
1993 *They're All The Same*, Centre for Contemporary Art, Ujazdoski Castle, Warsaw
The Only Good One is a Dead One, Matt's Gallery, London; Arnolfini, Bristol; Grey Art Gallery, New York University, New York

Ausgewählte Gruppenausstellungen/ Selected Group shows

2001-02 *Trauma*, Dundee Contemporary Arts, National Touring Exhibitions, Hayward Gallery tour to Colchester, Oxford and Nottingham
"Self" Portraits, Alexander and Bonin, New York
2000 *Hitchcock and Art: Fatal Coincidences*, Musée des Beaux-Arts de Montréal, Montreal
Landscape, British Council touring exhibition, ACC Gallery, Weimar, Germany and tour
1998 *Real/Life: New British Art*, Tochigi Prefectural Museum of Fine Arts; Fukouka City Art Museum; Hiroshima City Museum of Contemporary Art; Museum of Contemporary Art, Tokyo; Aishiya City Museum of Art and History, Japan
Wounds: between democracy and redemption in contemporary art, Moderna Museet, Stockholm
1997 *Pictura Britannica*, Museum of Contemporary Art, Sydney; Art Gallery of South Australia, Adelaide; Te Papa, Wellington, New Zealand
1996 10th Biennale of Sydney, Australia
1994 *Turner Prize*, Tate Gallery, London
1993 *An Irish Presence*, XLV Venice Biennale, Venice
1990 *The British Art Show 3*, London, Glasgow and Leeds

Ausgewählte Bibliographie/ Selected Bibliography

2001 *Willie Doherty*, Renaissance Society
Extracts from a File, DAAD/ Berliner Künstler-programm and Steidl Verlag, Göttingen
1998 *Dark Stains*, Koldo Mitexelena Kulturunea, San Sebastian, texts by Maite Lorés and Martin McLoone
Somewhere Else, Tate Gallery, Liverpool, text by Ian Hunt
1997 *same old story*, Matt's Gallery, London; Orchard Gallery, Derry; Firstsite, Colchester, texts by Martin McLoone and Jeffery Kastner
1996 *Willie Doherty*, Musée d'Art Moderne de la Ville de Paris, text by Olivier Zahm
The Only Good One is a Dead One, Fundaçeo Calouste Gulbenkian, Lisbon, Van Abbemuseum, Eindhoven
1994 *At the End of the Day*, British School at Rome, text by Carolyn Christov-Bakavgiev

Douglas Gordon

1966 Geboren / Born in Glasgow
1984-88 Glasgow School of Art
1988-90 The Slade School of Art, London
1996 Awarded the Turner Prize, Tate Gallery, London
Awarded Kunstpreis Niedersachsen, Kunstverein Hannover
1997 Awarded Premio 2000 at XLVII Venice Biennale
DAAD International Artists Programme, Berlin
1998 Awarded the Central Krankenversicherung Prize, Kölnischer Kunstverein, Cologne
Lord Provost's Award, Glasgow City Council, Glasgow
Awarded Guggenheim Museum SoHo Hugo Boss Prize, New York

Lebt und arbeitet / Lives and works in Glasgow

Ausgewählte Einzelausstellungen/ Selected Solo Exhibitions

2001 *Thirteen*, Gagosian Gallery, New York
2000 *Sheep and Goats*, Musée d'Art Moderne de la Ville de Paris, Paris
Tate Liverpool, Liverpool
Feature Film, Royal Festival Hall, London
1999 Centro Cultural de Belém, Lisbon
5 Year drive-by v. Bootleg (Empire), Neue Nationalgalerie, Berlin
Through a looking glass, XLVIII Venice Biennale, Venice
Feature Film, Artangel, Nuova Icona and Venice Biennale XLVIII, Venice
Feature Film, Artangel, at the Atlantis Gallery, London and Kunstverein, Cologne
1998 *Museet Project: Douglas Gordon*, Prästgården, Moderna Museet, Stockholm
Kunstverein Hannover, Hannover
1997 Biennale de Lyon, Lyon
Leben nach dem Leben nach dem Leben...., Deutsches Museum, Bonn
1996 *24 Hour Pyscho*, Akademie der Bildenden Künste, Vienna; Museum für Gegenwartskunst, Zurich

Ausgewählte Gruppenausstellungen/ Selected Group shows

2000 *Media City Seoul 2000*, Contemporary Art and Technology Biennial, Korea
Dream Machines, (curated by Susan Hiller), tour to London, Sheffield, Dundee
The British Art Show 5, Edinburgh, Southampton, Cardiff and Birmingham
New British Art 2000: Intelligence, Tate Britain, London
1999 Italian Pavilion, XLVIII Venice Biennale, Venice
1998 *Real/ Life, New British Art*, Tochigi Prefectural Museum of Fine Arts; Fukuoka City Art Museum; Hiroshima City Museum of Contemporary Art; Museum of Contemporary Art, Tokyo; Aishiya City Museum of Art and History, Japan
Berlin / Berlin, Berlin Biennale, Berlin, Germany
1997 *Past, Present, Future*, XLVII Venice Biennale, Venice
Pictura Britannica, Museum of Contemporary Art, Sydney, touring to the Art Gallery of South Australia, Adelaide; City Gallery, Wellington, New Zealand

1996 *Life/Live*, Musee d'Art de la Ville de Paris, Paris; Centro Cultural de Bélem, Lisbon
Manifesta 1, Rotterdam
Turner Prize, Tate Gallery, London
1995-96 *The British Art Show 4*, London, Manchester, Edinburgh and Cardiff
1995 *General Release*, British Council exhibition, Scuola di San Pasquale, Venice

Ausgewählte Bibliographie/ Selected Bibliography

1999 *Douglas Gordon: Kidnapping*, NAI Publishers, in association with Stedlijk Van Abbemuseum, Eindhoven, edited by Jan Debbaut and Marente Bloemheuvel
Feature Film: a book by Douglas Gordon, Artangel/ Book Works/ agnès b.
1998 *Douglas Gordon*, Kunstverein Hannover, texts by Eckhard Schneider, Lynne Cooke, Friedrich Meschede, Charles Esche
1993 *24 Hour Psycho*, Tramway, Glasgow, texts by Stuart Morgan and Ross Sinclair
Migrateurs, ARC Musée d'Art Moderne de la Ville de Paris, Paris, text by Douglas Gordon

Richard Hamilton

1922 Geboren / Born in London
1938-40 Royal Academy Schools
1946-47 resumed studies at Royal Academy Schools
1948-51 Slade School of Art
1960 Awarded the William and Norma Copley Foundation Prize for Painting
1969 Awarded John Moores Prize, London
1970 Awarded the Talins Prize International, Amsterdam
1974 DAAD, International Artists Programme, Berlin
1993 Awarded the Golden Lion of Venice, Venice

Lebt und arbeitet / Lives and works in Henley on Thames

Ausgewählte Einzelausstellungen/ Selected Solo Exhibitions

2001 24th International Biennial of Graphic Arts, Ljubljana, Slovenia
1998 *Richard Hamilton: Subject to an Impression*, Kunsthalle Bremen, Bremen
1993 British Pavilion, XLV Venice Biennale of Art, Venice
1992-93 Tate Gallery, London, and tour to Irish Museum of Modern Art, Dublin
1989 *teknologi <idé> konstverk*, Moderna Museet, Stockholm
1988 *Richard Hamilton, Work in Progress*, Orchard Gallery, Derry
1985 daadgalerie, Berlin
1983-84 *Image and Process*, Tate Gallery, London, and tour
1973 Guggenheim Museum, New York
1974 Städtische Galerie, Munich; Kunsthalle, Tübingen; Nationalgalerie, Berlin
1970 Tate Gallery, London
1955 *Man, Machine and Motion*, Institute of Contemporary Arts, London

Ausgewählte Gruppenausstellungen/ Selected Group shows

1997 Documenta X, Kassel
1991 *Pop Art*, Royal Academy of Arts, London; Museum Ludwig, Cologne, and Centro de Arte, Reina Sofia, Madrid
1990 *High and Low: Modern Art and Popular Culture*, Museum of Modern Art, New York
1989 São Paulo Biennial, São Paulo
1987 *British Art in the Twentieth Century*, Royal Academy, London
1983 *Aspects of Post-War Painting in Europe*, Solomon R. Guggenheim Museum, New York
1982 *Aspects of British Art Today*, Metropolitan Museum, Tokyo
1968 Documenta IV, Kassel
1956 *This is Tomorrow*, Whitechapel Art Gallery, London

Ausgewählte Bibliographie/ Selected Bibliography

1998 *Richard Hamilton*, Kunsthalle Bremen, Bremen, edited by Andreas Kreul, with texts by Jens Bove, Stephen Coppel, Wulf Herzogenrath, Andreas Kreul, Etienne Lullin and Dieter Schwarz and Richard Hamilton
1992 *Richard Hamilton*, Tate Gallery, London, texts by Richard Morphet, David Mellor, Sarat Maharaj, Stephen Snoddy
1988 *Richard Hamilton, Work in Progress*, Orchard Gallery, Derry, texts by Terry Eagleton and Richard Hamilton
1982 *Richard Hamilton, Collected Words*, Thames and Hudson, London

Damien Hirst

1965 Geboren / Born in Bristol
1989 Goldsmiths College, London
1994 DAAD, International Artists Programme, Berlin
1995 Awarded the Turner Prize, Tate Gallery, London
2001 Awarded the Gold Medal, Grand Prize, 24th International Biennial of Graphic Arts, Ljubljana

Lebt und arbeitet / Lives and works in Devon, England

Ausgewählte Einzelausstellungen/ Selected Solo Exhibitions

2000 *Theories, Models, Approaches, Assumptions, Results and Findings*, Gagosian Gallery, New York
1998 Southampton City Art Gallery, Southampton
1997 *Solo Exhibition*, Astrup Fearnley Museum, Oslo
The Beautiful Afterlife, Bruno Bischofberger, Zurich
No Sense of Absolute Corruption, Gagosian Gallery, New York
1995 *Still*, Jay Jopling / White Cube, London
1994 *A Good Environment for Coloured Monochrome Paintings*, DAAD Gallery, Berlin
1992 3rd Istanbul Biennale, Istanbul
Pharmacy, Cohen Gallery, New York

**Ausgewählte Gruppenausstellungen/
Selected Group shows**

2001   24th International Biennial of Graphic Arts, Ljubljana
Field Day: Sculpture from Britain, Taipei Fine Arts
Museum, Taiwan
Century City, Tate Modern, London

2000   *Sincerely Yours, British Art from the 90s*, Astrup
Fearnley Museum, Oslo

1997   *Sensation: Young British Artists from the Saatchi
Collection*, Royal Academy of Art, London; Hamburger
Bahnhof, Berlin; Brooklyn Museum of Art, New York

1998   *Pictura Britannica*, Museum of Contemporary Art,
Sydney; Art Gallery of South Australia, Adelaide;
City Gallery, Wellington, New Zealand

1996-97 *Live/Life*, Musee d'Art Moderne, Paris; Centro
Cultural de Bélem, Lisbon

1995   *Turner Prize*, Tate Gallery, London
Brilliant! Art from London, Walker Art Centre,
Minneapolis; Contemporary Arts Museum, Houston
British Art Show 4, London, Manchester, Edinburgh
and Cardiff
Minky Manky, South London Art Gallery; Arnolfini
Gallery, Bristol
Here and Now, Serpentine Gallery, London

1994   *Some Went Mad, Some Ran Away*, curated by Damien
Hirst, Serpentine Gallery, London; Nordic Arts Centre,
Helsinki; Kunstverein, Hannover; Museum of
Contemporary Art, Chicago; Portalen, Copenhagen

1993   *Aperto*, XLIII Venice Biennale, Venice

1988   *Freeze*, Surrey Docks, London

**Ausgewählte Bibliographie/
Selected Bibliography**

2000   *Theories, Models, Methods, Approaches, Results and
Findings*, Gagosian Gallery, New York and Science.
Edited by Damien Hirst and Jason Beard, with texts
by Gordon Burn and George Poste

1997   *I Want to Spend the Rest of My Life Everywhere,
With Everyone, One to One, Always, Forever, Now*,
Booth-Clibborn Editions, London

1996   *No Sense of Absolute Corruption*, Gagosian Gallery,
New York, interview by Stuart Morgan

1991   *Damien Hirst*, the Institute of Contemporary Arts,
London and Jay Jopling, London, texts by Iwona
Blazwick, Charles Hall, interview by Sophie Calle

Steve McQueen

1969   Geboren / Born in London
1989-90 Chelsea School of Art, London
1990-93 Goldsmiths College, London
1993-94 Tisch School of the Arts, New York University, New York
1996   ICA Futures Award, London
1998   DAAD International Artists Programme, Berlin
1999   Awarded the Turner Prize, Tate Gallery, London

Lebt und arbeitet / Lives and works in Amsterdam

**Ausgewählte Einzelausstellungen/
Selected Solo Exhibitions**

2001   Kunsthalle Wien, Vienna

Museu de Arte Moderna São Paulo
Museo Rufino Tamayo, Mexico

2000   *Barrage*, daadgalerie, Berlin
Cold Breath, Delfina Projects, London
Marian Goodman Gallery, New York
Sala Mendoza, Caracas
Institute for Contemporary Art, Cape Town

1999   Institute of Contemporary Arts, London
Kunsthalle, Zurich

1998   Boijmans van Beuningen Museum, Rotterdam
Four projected images, Museum of Modern Art,
San Francisco
Galerie Marian Goodman, Paris

1997   Portikus, Frankfurt
Stedelijk van Abbemuseum, Eindhoven
Milwaukee Art Museum, Milwaukee
Museum of Modern Art, New York

1996   Museum of Contemporary Art, Chicago
Anthony Reynolds Gallery, London

**Ausgewählte Gruppenausstellungen/
Selected Group shows**

1999   *Turner Prize Exhibition*, Tate Gallery, London
1998   *Wounds: between democracy and redemption in
contemporary art*, Moderna Museet, Stockholm
1997   Documenta 10, Kassel, Germany
2nd Johannesburg Biennale, Johannesburg
1996-97 *Live/Life*, Musee d'Art Moderne, Paris; Centro Cultural
de Bélem, Lisbon
1996   *Spellbound*, Hayward Gallery, London
1995   *The British Art Show 4*, London, Manchester, Edinburgh
and Cardiff

**Ausgewählte Bibliographie/
Selected Bibliography**

2001   Steve McQueen, Kunsthalle Wien, Vienna
1999   *Steve McQueen*, Institute of Contemporary Arts,
London and Kunsthalle, Zurich, texts by Michael
Newman, Robert Storr and Okwui Enwezor
1997   *Steve McQueen*, Portikus, Frankfurt
1996   *Steve McQueen*, Museum of Contemporary Art, Chicago

Vong Phaophanit

1961   Geboren / Born in Savannakhet, Laos
1980-85 Ecole des Beaux Arts, Aix en Provence, France
1993   Nomination for the Turner Prize, Tate Gallery, London
1996-97 DAAD International Artists Programme, Berlin

Lebt und arbeitet / Lives and works in London

**Ausgewählte Einzelausstellungen/
Selected Solo Exhibitions**

2001   Asia Society, New York
Bath City Centre and Spa Redevelopment Project
1999   Stephen Friedman Gallery, London
1998   *Atopia*, Royal Festival Hall, South Bank Centre, London
1997   *Atopia*, daadgalerie, Berlin
1996   Stephen Friedman Gallery, London

1995 *Phaophanit and Piper*, Angel Row Gallery, Nottingham;
   Site Gallery, Sheffield; Cambridge
   Darkroom, Cambridge; The Minories, Colchester
1993 *Ash and Silk Wall*, Greenwich Thames Barrier Park
   Project, London
   permanent sculpture commissioned by Greenwich
   Borough Council and Public Art Development Trust
1991-92 *tok tem dean kep kin bo dai (what falls to the ground*
   but can't be eaten), Chisenhale Gallery, London, adapt-
   ed for showing at the Ikon Gallery, Birmingham

Ausgewählte Gruppenausstellungen/
Selected Group Exhibitions

1999 *3rd Asia-Pacific Triennial*, Queensland Art Gallery,
   Brisbane, Australia
1997 *Pictura Britannica*, Museum of Contemporary Art,
   Sydney; Art Gallery of South Australia, Adelaide;
   City Gallery, Wellington, New Zealand
1995 *Here and Now*, Serpentine Gallery, London
1993 *Neon Rice Field*, *Turner Prize*, Tate Gallery, London
   Four Rooms, Serpentine Gallery, London
   Aperto, XLV Venice Biennale of Art, Venice
   Prospect '93, Kunstverein, Frankfurt
1990 *The British Art Show 3*, Glasgow, Leeds and London.

Ausgewählte Bibliographie/
Selected Bibliography

1995 *Phaophanit and Piper*, published by Eddie Chambers,
   Bristol
   Vong Phaophanit, De Appel, Amsterdam
1992 Public Art Development Trust, London
1991 *tok tem dean kep kin bo dai (what falls to the ground*
   but can't be eaten), Chisenhale Gallery, London and
   Ikon Gallery, Birmingham

Richard Wentworth

1947 Geboren / Born in Samoa
1965 Hornsey College of Art, London
1966-70 Royal College of Art, London
1974 Mark Rothko Memorial Award
1993-94 DAAD, International Artists Programme, Berlin
1998 Curator of *Richard Wentworth's Thinking Aloud*,
   National Touring Exhibition, tour to Cambridge,
   Manchester and London

   Lebt und arbeitet / Lives and works in London

Ausgewählte Einzelausstellungen/
Selected Solo Exhibitions

2000 Galerie Margaret Biedermann, Munich
1999 Lisson Gallery, London
   The Visit, Galleri Wang, Oslo
1998 Kunstverein Freiburg, toured to Städtische Galerie
   Groeppingen; Bonner Kunstverein, Germany
1997 Monica de Cardenas Gallery, Milan
1996 *Little Differences: Richard Wentworth at the Christ*
   Church Picture Gallery, Christ Church Picture Gallery,
   Oxford
1995 Lisson Gallery, London

1994 *Travelling without a Map*, Kunstwerke, daadgalerie, Berlin
   Musée des Beaux Arts et de la Dentelle, Calais
   Museum het Kruithuis, Stedeljik Museum Voor
   Hedndaagse Kunst, 's-Hertogenbosche, Holland
   Arnolfini, Bristol
1993 Serpentine Gallery, London

Ausgewählte Gruppenausstellungen/
Selected Group Exhibitions

2001 *Field Day: Sculpture from Britain*, Taipei Fine Art
   Museum, Taiwan
1996-97 *Live/Life*, Musee d'Art Moderne, Paris; Centro
   Cultural de Bélem, Lisbon
1995 4th Istanbul Biennal, Istanbul
   Here and Now, Serpentine Gallery, London
1990 Biennale of Sydney, Sydney, Australia
1984 *The British Art Show 2*, Birmingham, Edinburgh,
   Sheffield and Southampton

Ausgewählte Bibliographie/
Selected Bibliography

1997 *Richard Wentworth*, Kunstverein Freiburg im Marien-
   bad, Städtische Galerie Göppingen, Bonner Kunstverein. Texts by Gregor Muir, Stephan Berg, Werner
   Meyer and Richard Wentworth
1994 *Berlin 117 Landmarks/ Marksteine*, Berliner Künstlerprogramm, DAAD, Berlin
   Richard Wentworth, Musée des Beaux-Arts, Calais,
   text by Marina Warner
1993 *Richard Wentworth*, Thames & Hudson, London,
   in association with the Serpentine Gallery, London.
   Texts by Andrea Schlieker and Marina Warner

Rachel Whiteread

1963 Geboren / Born in London
1982-85 Brighton Polytechnic, Brighton
1985-87 Slade School of Fine Art, London
1992-93 DAAD International Artists Programme, Berlin
1993 Awarded the Turner Prize, Tate Gallery, London

   Lebt und arbeitet / Lives and works in London

Ausgewählte Einzelausstellungen/
Selected Solo Exhibitions

2001 Scottish National Gallery of Modern Art, Edinburgh
   Serpentine Gallery, London
   Fourth Plinth Project, Trafalgar Square, London
2000 *Holocaust Memorial*, Judenplatz, Vienna
1998 *Water Tower Project*, Public Art Fund, New York
1997 Reina Sofia, Madrid
   British Pavilion, XLVII Venice Biennale of Art, Venice
   Shedding Life, Tate Gallery, Liverpool
1995 *Sculptures*, British School at Rome
1994 *Skulpturen/Sculptures*, Kunsthalle, Basel; Institute
   of Contemporary Art, Philadelphia; Institute of
   Contemporary Art, Boston
1993 *Sculptures*, Museum of Contemporary Art, Chicago
   House, commissioned by Artangel Trust and Beck's, London
   Zeichnungen, daadgalerie, Berlin

Ausgewählte Gruppenausstellungen/ Selected Group Exhibitions

2001 *Field Day: Sculpture from Britain*, Taipei Fine Arts Museum, Taiwan

2000 *Sincerely Yours: British Art from the 90s*, Astrup Fearnley Museum of Modern Art, Oslo, Norway

1998-99 *Real/Life, New British Art*, Tochigi Prefectural Museum of Fine Arts; Fukuoka City Art Museum; Hiroshima City Museum of Contemporary Art; Museum of Contemporary Art, Tokyo; Aishiya City Museum of Art and History, Japan

1998 *Wounds: between democracy and redemption in contemporary art*, Moderna Museet, Stockholm

1997 *Sensation: Young British Artists from the Saatchi Collection*, Royal Academy of Arts, London; Hamburger Bahnhof, Berlin; Brooklyn Museum of Art, Brooklyn, New York

1995 *Brilliant! New Art from London*, Walker Art Centre, Minneapolis and Museum of Fine Arts, Houston
4th Istanbul Biennal, Istanbul
Here and Now, Serpentine Gallery, London

1993 *Turner Prize*, Tate Gallery, London

1991 *Metropolis*, Martin Gropius Bau, Berlin

1990 *British Art Show 3*, Glasgow, Leeds and London

Ausgewählte Bibliographie/ Selected Bibliography

2001 *Rachel Whiteread*, Scottish National Gallery of Modern Art, Edinburgh, and the Serpentine Gallery, London. Texts by Patrick Elliott, Lisa Corrin and Andrea Schlieker

2000 *Judenplatz: Place of Remembrance*, Museum Judenplatz Vienna, Pichler Verlag, text by Andrea Schlieker

1998 *Rachel Whiteread*, Anthony d'Offay Gallery, London, text by A.M Homes

1997 *Rachel Whiteread*, XLVII Venice Biennale, The British Council, interview by Andrea Rose
Shedding Life, Tate Gallery Liverpool, texts by Rosalind Krauss, Bartolomeu Mari, Stuart Morgan, Fiona Bradley and Michael Tarantino

1995 *House*, Phaidon Press Ltd., London, texts by John Bird, John Davies, James Lingwood, Doreen Massey, Ian Sinclair, Richard Shone, Neil Thomas, Anthony Vidler and Simon Watney

Stephen Willats

1943 Geboren / Born in London
1962-63 Ealing School of Art, London
1965- Editor and publisher of *Control Magazine*
1972-73 Director of the Centre for Behavioural Art, London
1979-80 DAAD International Artists Programme, Berlin

Lebt und arbeitet / Lives and works in London

Ausgewählte Einzelausstellungen/ Selected Solo Exhibitions

2000 *Macro to Micro*, Gallery Laure Genillard, London
1998 *Parallele Begegnungen an verschiedenen Orten*, Gesellschaft für Aktuelle Kunst, Bremen

Concepts, Strategies and Models, 1962 – 65, Gimpel Fils, London
Multicult Berlin, Galerie Franck & Schulte, Berlin
Changing Everything, South London Art Gallery
Random Encounter, Southampton City Art Gallery

1997 *Street Talk*, Victoria Miro Gallery, London

1995 *Living Together*, Tramway, Glasgow

1994 *Fateful Combinations*, The British School at Rome
Museum Mosaic, Tate Gallery, Liverpool

1993 *Multiple Clothing*, Institute of Contemporary Arts, London
Buildings & People, Berlinische Galerie, Berlin; Goethe Institute, London

1986 *Concepts and Models*, Institute of Contemporary Arts, London

1980-81 *4 Inseln in Berlin*, National Galerie, Berlin; Goethe Institute, London

1979-80 *Concerning our Present Way of Living*, Whitechapel Art Gallery, London; Stedelijk Van Abbemuseum, Eindhoven

Ausgewählte Gruppenausstellungen/ Selected Group Exhibitions

2001 *City Racing: A Partial Account*, Institute of Contemporary Arts, London

2000 *Protest and Survive*, Whitechapel Art Gallery, London
Live in Your Head, Whitechapel Art Gallery, London; Museo do Chiado, Lisbon

1995 *Imprint 93*, City Racing, London

1993 *Sixties Art Scene in London*, Barbican Art Gallery, London

1991 *Shocks to the System*, Arts Council of Great Britain touring exhibition, South Bank Centre, London

1982 *Aperto*, XL Venice Biennale, Venice

Ausgewählte Bibliographie/ Selected Bibliography

2001 *Multichannel Vision*, Control, London

2000 *Multiple Clothing*, Walther König, Cologne
Art and Social Function (Reprint of 1976 original), Ellipsis, London

1998 *Random Encounter*, Southampton City Art Gallery

1996 *Between Buildings and People*, Academy Editions, London

1995 *Wie ich meine Fluchtwege organisiere*, Edition 931, Leipzig

1976 *Art and Social Function*, Latimer New Dimensions,London

1973 *The Artist As An Instigator of Changes in Social Cognition and Behaviour*, Gallery House Press, London

Jane & Louise Wilson

1967 Geboren in Newcastle / Born in Newcastle
1986-89 Duncan of Jordanstone College of Art (Louise)
Newcastle Polytechnic (Jane)
1990-92 Goldsmiths College, London (Jane & Louise)
1993 Barclays Young Artist Award
1999 DAAD International Artists Programme, Berlin/ Hanover
Nomination for the Turner Prize, Tate Gallery, London
2000 IASPIS, International Artists Studio Program in Sweden, Stockholm Residency

Leben und arbeiten / Live and work in London

Einzelausstellungen/
Two-Person Exhibitions

2000 *Star-City*, 303 Gallery, New York
Parliament, Bernier/Eliades, Athens
Stasi City & Crawl Space, MIT List Visual Arts Centre, Cambridge, MA
1999 *Gamma*, Lisson Gallery, London
Stasi City, Hamburger Kunsthalle, Hamburg
Jane and Louise Wilson, Serpentine Gallery, London
1997 *Stasi City*, Kunstverein Hannover; Kunstraum Munich; Centre d'Art Contemporain, Geneva; Kunstwerke, Berlin
Jane and Louise Wilson, LEA, London
1995 *Normapaths*, Chisenhale Gallery, London and tour
Crawl Space, Milch Gallery, London

Ausgewählte Gruppenausstellungen/
Selected Group Exhibitions

2001 *Public Offerings*, LA MOCA, Los Angeles
2000 *Dream Machines*, (curated by Susan Hiller), tour to Dundee, Sheffield and London
Turner Prize, Tate Gallery, London
1999 *Trace*, Liverpool Biennial, Tate Gallery Liverpool
1997 *Pictura Britannica*, Museum of Contemporary Art, Sydney, touring to the Art Gallery of South Australia, Adelaide; City Gallery, Wellington, New Zealand
1995 *British Art Show 4*, Edinburgh, Manchester, Cardiff
General Release, Scuola San Pasquale, Venice
Here and Now, Serpentine Gallery, London

Ausgewählte Bibliographie/
Selected Bibliography

2001 *Jane & Louise Wilson*, Ellipsis, London, in association with the Film and Video Umbrella, London, texts by Jeremy Millar and Claire Doherty
1999 *Jane & Louise Wilson*, Serpentine Gallery, text by Peter Schjeldahl, interview by Lisa Corrin
1996 *Stasi City*, Kunstverein Hannover
1995 *Normapaths*, Chisenhale Gallery, London, text by Cherry Smyth

On Site, Museet for Samtidskunst, Oslo
1990 *Take Away*, Centre for Contemporary Art, Warsaw
1989 *High Rise*, XX São Paulo Bienal, São Paulo
1987 *20:50*, Matt's Gallery, London

Ausgewählte Gruppenausstellungen/
Selected Group Exhibitions

2001 *Field Day: Sculpture from Britain*, Taipei Fine Art Museum, Taiwan
2000 *Structurally Sound*, Ex Teresa Arte Actual, Mexico City, Mexico
1996 *Mirades (sobre el Museu)*, MACBA, Barcelona
Islands, National Gallery of Australia, Canberra
1993 *A Space without Art*, Fernsehturm, Berlin
1992 *Boundary Rider*, IX Sydney Biennial, Sydney
Another World, Mito Foundation, Tokyo

Öffentliche Arbeiten
Permanent Public Works

2001 A sculpture for the Millennium Square, Leeds
Final Corner, World Cup Project, Fukuroi City, Japan
2000 *Set North for Japan 74°. 33.2"*, Nakasato Village, Niigata
1999 *Over Easy*, The Arc, Stockton-on-Tees
1994 Entrance to the Utility Tunnel, Tachikawa Art Project, Tokyo

Ausgewählte Bibliographie/
Selected Bibliography

2001 *Richard Wilson*, Merrell Publishing, London, text by Michael Archer, Simon Morrisey and Harry Stocks
1999 *Turbine Hall Swimming Pool*, Café Gallery Projects
1996 *Jamming Gears*, Serpentine Gallery, text by Andrew Wilson
1994 *Deep End*, British Council and the MOCA, Los Angeles, interview by Paul Schimmel
1993 *Richard Wilson*, DAAD Künstlerprogramm, Berlin, text by James Roberts
1989 *Richard Wilson*, Matt's Gallery in association with MOMA Oxford/ and the Arnolfini, Bristol, text by Michael Newman

Richard Wilson

1953 Geboren / Born in London
1970-71 London College of Printing
1971-74 Hornsey College of Art
1974-76 Reading University
1992 DAAD International Artists Programme, Berlin

Lebt und arbeitet / Lives and works in London

Ausgewählte Einzelausstellungen/
Selected Solo Exhibitions

2000 *Slice of Reality*, Millennium Dome Sculpture Project, London
Turbine Hall Swimming Pool, Clare College Mission Church, London
1996 *Jamming Gears*, Serpentine Gallery, London
1993 Museum of Contemporary Art, Los Angeles

Victor Burgin
NIETZSCHE'S PARIS, 1999
single screen video projection
DVD 8 minute programme loop, colour, NTSC stereo
Courtesy of the artist

Mat Collishaw
INFECTIOUS FLOWERS II, 1996
lightbox with photographic transparency
3 pieces, 50 x 50 x 10 cm each
Collection Ivor Braka & Thomas Dane

SHANGRI LA, 2001
video installation
acrylic, steel, cloth
240 x 130 x 130 cm
Courtesy Modern Art, London

Tacita Dean
FERNSEHTURM, 2001
16 mm-film, optical sound, 44 minutes
Courtesy of the artist, Frith Street Gallery, London,
and Marian Goodman Gallery New York/Paris

Willie Doherty
EXTRACTS FROM A FILE, 2000
black and white photographs mounted on aluminium
45 x 60 cm each
Courtesy Galerie Peter Kilchmann, Zurich

Douglas Gordon
FROM THE MOMENT YOU READ THESE
WORDS UNTIL YOU MEET SOMEONE WITH BLUE EYES, 1993
wall mounted text
Collection Mario Codognato and
Mirta d'Argenzio, Rome

WHAT YOU WANT ME TO SAY, 1998
sound installation
12" vinyl disc, 1 record player, 12 speakers, 12 sound cables,
3 amplifiers
Collection Migros Museum für Gegenwartskunst, Zurich

Richard Hamilton
THE PASSAGE OF THE BRIDE, 1998-99
painting, oil on cibachrome on canvas
102 x 127 cm
Courtesy Richard Hamilton

BATHROOM FIG. 1, 1999
painting, oil on cibachrome on canvas
50 x 50 cm
Courtesy Rita Donagh

BATHROOM FIG. 2, 1999/2000
painting, oil on cibachrome on canvas
100 x 100 cm
Courtesy Richard Hamilton

Damien Hirst
Yikes, 1997
glass, mdf and drug packaging
38 x 76 cm
Collection Jonathan Barnbrook, London

Pseudechis Colletti Guttatus, 2000
gloss household paint on canvas
114.3 x 160 cm
Courtesy Anne Faggionato, London

Naja Naja Kaouthia, 2000
household gloss on canvas
246 x 251.5 cm
Collection of Hugh Allan, London

Stripteaser, 1996
glass/steel wall cabinet
six parts filled with skeletons and surgical instruments
195.2 x 420 x 48 cm
Collection of the artist

Steve McQueen
Five Easy Pieces, 1995
video installation, 16 mm b/w and colour film/
video transfer
7.34 minutes duration
Courtesy Marian Goodman Gallery, New York
and Paris,
Courtesy Thomas Dane Ltd., London

Vong Phaophanit
Atopia, 2001
steel shelving, polybutadeine synthetic rubber
300 x 300 x 200 cm
Courtesy Vong Phaophanit and
Stephen Friedman Gallery, London

Richard Wentworth
Making Do & Getting By, 1976-99
framed photographs
43.5 x 51 cm each
Courtesy Lisson Gallery, London

Spread, 1997
ceramic
6 m diameter
Courtesy Lisson Gallery, London

Rachel Whiteread
Untitled (24 switches), 1998
aluminium
26.3 x 20.3 x 6 cm
Private Collection

Untitled (Stories), 1998
polystyrene and plaster
99 x 120 x 26 cm
Private Collection

Untitled (Cast Corridor), 2000
cast iron (24 units)
1.5 x 226 x 405 cm
Courtesy Collection Robert R. Littman and Sully Bonnelly

Untitled (Six Spaces), 1996
resin
51 x 38 x 38 cm each
Courtesy Arts Council Collection, Hayward Gallery, London

Jane and Louise Wilson
Star City, 2000
four screen video installation
screens 410 x 310 cm each
Courtesy Lisson Gallery, London, and 303 Gallery, New York

Richard Wilson
Bottom Drawer 1, 2000
metal filing cabinet
133 x 75 x 55 cm
Courtesy Richard Wilson

Bottom Drawer 2, 2001
metal filing cabinet
133 x 62 x 47 cm
Courtesy Richard Wilson

Bottom Drawer 3, 2001
metal filing cabinet
133 x 62 x 47 cm
Courtesy Richard Wilson

Stephen Willats
Wie ich meine Fluchtwege organisiere, 1979/80
4 photo panel work
photographic prints, letraset text, mixed media on card,
framed with perspex
82.5 x 128 cm each
Courtesy the artist and Galerie Thomas Schulte, Berlin

Wie ich entdecke, dass wir
von andern abhängig sind,
1979/80
3 photo panel work
photographs, letraset text, mixed media on card,
framed with perspex
130 x 98 cm each
Courtesy the artist and Galerie Thomas Schulte, Berlin

Eine Postmoderne Lebensform, 1992/93
2 photo panel work
photographs, acrylic paint, letraset text and mixed media
126 x 76.5 cm each
Courtesy the artist and Galerie Thomas Schulte, Berlin

Von einer Generation zur nächsten, 1992/93
2 photo panel work
photographs, acrylic paint, letraset text and mixed media
76.5 x 127 cm each
Courtesy the artist and Galerie Thomas Schulte, Berlin

Leihgeber / Lenders

Hugh Allan, London
Jonathan Barnbrook, London
Ivor Braka & Thomas Dane
Victor Burgin
Mario Codognato and Mirta d'Argenzio, Rome
Thomas Dane Ltd., London
Tacita Dean
Rita Donagh
Anne Faggionato
Frith Street Gallery, London
Marian Goodman Gallery, New York/Paris
Richard Hamilton
Damien Hirst
Lisson Gallery, London
Robert R. Littman and Sully Bonnelly
Migros Museum für Gegenwartskunst, Zürich
Modern Art, London
Galerie Peter Kilchmann, Zürich
Arts Council Collection, Hayward Gallery, London
Richard Wilson
Stephen Willats
Galerie Thomas Schulte, Berlin

Andrea Schlieker möchte danken / would like to thank:

Friedrich Meschede, DAAD Berlin, für die Initiierung der Ausstellung / for initiating the exhibition;
Andrea Rose, Brett Rogers, Tamsin Godfrey und besonders / and especially Ann Gallagher, British Council London, / für Rat und Unterstützung / for advice and support;
Ruth Ur, British Council London, für ihre Hilfe bei der Ausstellung im allgemeinen und der Zusammenstellung der Künstlerbiografien im besonderen / for her help with the exhibition in general and for compiling all artists' biographies in particular;
Tony Andrews und /and Elke Ritt, British Council Berlin;
Sue McDiarmid für ihre kompetente Installation aller Film- und Videoarbeiten / for the expert handling of all the video and film installations' technical complexities;
Peter Nils Dorén für die ideenreiche Gestaltung des Katalogs / for his imaginative design of the catalogue;
Tim Llewellyn, The Henry Moore Foundation, für die Mitfinanzierung des Katalogs / for kickstarting the funding of the catalogue;
Richard Blythe für sein aufmerksames Lesen des Textes / for his attentive reading of the manuscript;
Clarrie Wallis, Tate Britain, für ihre Hilfe beim Transfer von 'Fernsehturm' von London nach Leipzig / for her help with transferring 'Fernsehturm' from London to Leipzig;
Beatrice von Bismarck, für Berlin-Leipzig-London Gespräche / for Berlin-Leipzig-London conversations;
Klaus Werner, ehemaliger Direktor der GfZK, für seinen Enthusiasmus, an diesem Projekt teilzunehmen / former director of the GfZK Leipzig, for his enthusiasm to participate in this project;
Barbara Steiner, Jan Winkelmann, GfZK Leipzig, für die Präsentation von DoubleVision in ihren schönen Räumen / for presenting the exhibition in their beautiful space;
der kompetenten technischen Leitung von / the expert technical management of Jürgen and Angela Böhnke,
sowie allen Aufbauhelfern für ihr Durchhaltevermögen / as well as the entire technical team for their staying power:
Frank Lustig, Uwe Karsten Günther, Frank Dopmeier, Uwe Schulze, Bert Watler, Francis Hunger, Rene Pölzing, Denis Lucé, Rigo Schmidt;
Simone Schmidt für Feinfühligkeit und Ausdauer / for sensitivity and patience;
allen Leihgebern / all lenders to the exhibition;
den Galerien der Künstler für eine fruchtbare Zusammenarbeit / the artists' galleries for a fruitful collaboration;
besonders / especially Simon Preston at Thomas Dane Ltd; Suzanna Greeves and Jennifer Thatcher at Anthony d'Offay Gallery; Patricia Kohl at Stephen Friedmann Gallery; Rose Lord and Dale McFarland at Frith Street Gallery; Pilar Corrias and Jari Lager at Lisson Gallery; Heidi MacLeod at Modern Art; Hugh Allen at Science; Irene Bradbury at White Cube;
und ganz besonders den Künstlern für ihr Engagement und Vertrauen / and especially all the artists for their trust and commitment.

Katalog veröffentlicht aus Anlass der Ausstellung DOUBLE VISION, Galerie für Zeitgenössische Kunst, Leipzig, 23. Juni bis 12. August 2001 / Catalogue published to coincide with the exhibition DOUBLE VISION at the Galerie für Zeitgenössische Kunst, Leipzig, 23 June to 12 August 2001.

Ausstellung kuratiert von / Exhibition curated by
Andrea Schlieker, London

DOUBLE VISION gemeinschaftlich finanziert von /
DOUBLE VISION is jointly funded by
The British Council, London,
Berliner Künstlerprogramm DAAD, Berlin,
Galerie für Zeitgenössische Kunst, Leipzig,
mit zusätzlicher Unterstützung von / with additional support from
The British Council, Berlin.

Der Katalog wurde großzügig unterstützt /
This catalogue has been generously funded by
The Henry Moore Foundation,
mit zusätzlicher Unterstützung vom /
with additional support from
DAAD, Berlin, and The British Council, London.

Herausgegeben von / Edited by Andrea Schlieker

Übersetzung / Translation: Cornelia C. Walter, Berlin
Design: Dorén + Köster, Berlin
Druck / Printed by: Druckerei Gerike, Berlin
Lithography: MegaSatzService, Berlin
Auflage / edition: 1000

© Andrea Schlieker 2001 © Die Künstler / The artists
© DAAD, Berlin

Umschlagabbildung / Cover image:
Richard Hamilton, The passage of the bride, 1998-99

Photographen-Verzeichnis / Photographic credits:
Die Künstler / The artists, Mike Bruce, Theo Coulombe,
Peter Nils Dorén, Heidi Kosaniuk, Friedrich Meschede,
Mike Parsons, Stephen White, Werner Zellien, Jens Ziehe

ISBN 3-89357-097-7